Juan Domingo Perón:
A History

———————

Juan Domingo Perón:
A History

Robert J. Alexander

Westview Press / Boulder, Colorado

Copyright © 1979 by Westview Press, Inc.

Published in 1979 in the United States of America by
  Westview Press, Inc.
  5500 Central Avenue
  Boulder, Colorado 80301
  Frederick A. Praeger, Publisher

Library of Congress Cataloging in Publication Data
Alexander, Robert Jackson, 1918-
  Juan Domingo Perón: A History
  Bibliography: p.
  Includes index.
  1. Perón, Juan Domingo, Pres. Argentine Republic, 1895-1974. 2. Argentine Republic—Presidents—Biography. 3. Argentine Republic—History—1943-
4. Peronism.
F2849.P48A59   982'.06-0924 [B]   78-21705
ISBN 0-89158-364-5

Printed and bound in the United States of America

To Jock and Mary Powell

Contents

Preface

This is not the first volume that I have written about Juan Perón. The first book I ever published, *The Perón Era*, which came out in September 1951, was one of the earliest studies in English of the Perón phenomenon. However, it was written at the height of the Argentine leader's power, and most of Perón's political career was still to come.

At this writing, Perón has been dead for more than three years. It is now possible to present at least a tentative assessment of his overall importance in his own country and in the American Hemisphere. This book attempts to do so.

The present volume is an interpretative essay rather than a scholarly treatise. Therefore, it is unencumbered by the paraphernalia of footnotes and other scholarly impedimenta. However, at the end of the book there is a bibliographic note indicating both my principal sources and other volumes that might be used by readers who want to explore the phenomenon of Juan Domingo Perón further.

I have followed the career of Juan Perón more or less at first hand since the first few months he was in power. I first visited Argentina late in 1946 soon after Perón had become president for the first time. I was there three other times while he was still in power, and nine times after 1955 when he was ousted. I have thus been able to observe the evolution of Argentina over almost a third of a century. This book is based largely on those observations.

During this period of observation, I had a chance to talk with a large number of people who participated in the Perón experience, either as his friends or as his opponents. Included among those with whom I talked was Juan Perón himself; I interviewed Perón in 1960. I directly refer to that interview and a few others in the pages that follow.

Of course, I owe many debts to people who have contributed directly or indirectly to this book. Over more than thirty years, I talked with nearly a thousand different people—many of whom I interviewed several times—and they did much to educate me about Argentina. I cannot mention them individually, but I wish to thank them anyway. In addition, I am much obliged to the editors of Westview Press for their help in transforming the manuscript into a book.

I also owe a particular debt of gratitude to my wife, Joan Alexander, who has not only borne with my working on this book, but has also given me extremely helpful editorial advice about it. Joan knows a great deal about Argentina; she was an exceedingly valuable adviser in the preparation of this work.

Of course, no one is responsible for whatever is wrong with this book except its author. I am therefore answerable for any errors of fact or interpretation which may appear in the pages that follow.

One final note to those who may find the chronology of succeeding Argentine presidents mentioned in this book to be somewhat confusing. Appendix A, which lists the Argentine presidents between 1916 and 1977, may be consulted for the dates of their incumbency, and how they assumed and left office.

Robert J. Alexander
Rutgers University

Abbreviations

ATLAS	Agrupación de Trabajadores Latino Americanos Sindicalizados
CGE	Confederación General Económica
CGP	Confederación General de Profesionales
CGT	Confederación General del Trabajo
CORA	Confederación Obrera Regional Argentina
ERP	Ejército Revolucionario del Pueblo
FORA	Federación Obrera Regional Argentina
GOU	Grupo de Oficiales Unidos
IAPI	Instituto Argentino de Producción e Intercambio
MID	Movimiento de Integración y Desarrollo
UES	Unión de Estudiantes Secundarios
USA	Unión Sindical Argentina
YPF	Yacimientos Petroliferos Fiscales

ONE

Pre-Perón Argentina

Juan Domingo Perón was what Latin Americans often like to call a *fenómeno*. We might translate that best in English as a "paradox." He was a soldier who became the boss and idol of a trade union movement that had a long history of opposition to the armed forces and to militarism in general. He divided the public opinion of his country more deeply and more bitterly than anyone in a hundred years, but when he returned to power after almost a generation he came as a symbol of unity and reconciliation. He was forced to live eighteen years in exile, having little personal contact with his rank and file followers, but nonetheless he was able to maintain the strongest hold on their loyalty. He saw himself as a leader of major significance, but so successfully destroyed any subordinate figure who might possibly challenge his position that he left an inheritance of an almost leaderless political movement, the survival of which was highly problematical. He carried out economic and social policies that were long overdue, but he left his country in the grip of perhaps the worst economic crisis of its history.

Perón came from a relatively modest provincial background. He chose military life early, going to the National Military Academy, graduating in 1915, pursuing a somewhat plodding army career, and only reaching the rank of colonel a couple of years before the Revolution of June 4, 1943. That event launched his political career and brought his quick emergence as a popularly elected president of the Republic in June 1946. He stayed in office after reelection in 1951 until he was overthrown by a military uprising in September 1955. The

1

following eighteen years were spent in exile, but Perón never gave up his efforts to return to Argentina and to power. These efforts culminated in his triumphant homecoming in June 1973, followed shortly by his election once again as president of the Republic. However, by the time of his triumph he was already mortally ill, and he died less than nine months after his inauguration.

The Early Evolution of Argentina

In order to understand the paradox of Perón one must start by knowing something about Argentina as it existed before Perón strode across its political stage. Only then can one begin to comprehend what he did, why he did it, and why it came out as it did.

Argentina was a relatively unimportant part of the Spanish Empire. Most of it remained in the hands of the Indians and of the Indians' most bitter adversaries, the mestizo (half-breed) gauchos or cowboys. A scattering of small cities in the interior conducted trade over the mountains with Bolivia and Peru, and Buenos Aires was a center for modest trade (much of it smuggling) with the littoral.

The country did not change substantially during the first generation of independence, which occurred in the second decade of the nineteenth century. During much of that time it was ruled by a collection of *caudillos,* provincial despots, the most outstanding of whom was Juan Manuel de Rosas, the tyrant of the province of Buenos Aires. For all practical purposes, a national government did not even exist much of the time.

It was not until after the overthrow of Rosas in 1852 that the country began to achieve national unity and to be transformed economically and socially. The formation of a single nation was only achieved after two short civil wars between Buenos Aires and the rest of the country. A federal republic with jurisdiction over most of the national territory laid the groundwork for Argentina's rapid economic development during the decades surrounding the turn of the nineteenth century. By the 1860s the pattern of rural landownership that had evolved during the long struggle with the Indians, which still largely persists, had been established. Rosas and other caudillos, as well as their successors in the unified government, carried on a relentless war with the aborigines. This "conquest of the desert," as the Argentines are prone to call it, was virtually completed by the beginning of the 1880s.

As land was taken from the Indians, it was given by successive governments to new white and mestizo landlords. In theory, the land was apportioned largely among those who had fought in the wars against the Indians, the amount of land each person received being dependent on his rank in the military or his influence with the political powers. In practice, most subordinate personnel had no resources with which to develop the land given to them, and they tended to sell it to the larger grantees. As a result, by the 1860s most of the great fertile pampa belt centering on Buenos Aires had been divided among a relatively small number of very large landowners. Much the same happened farther south, in Patagonia, which also was wrested from the control of the Indians.

From the 1860s on, deliberate government policy, aided by important technological developments, transformed the economy and society of Argentina. A series of presidents in the period of the 1860s through the 1880s sought to develop the agricultural and grazing potentialities of the pampas and Patagonia. To this end, they encouraged the building of railroads ·capable of transporting meat and grains to the two principal ports of Buenos Aires and Rosario. At the same time, the national leaders sought to modernize these and other important cities, providing them with the infrastructures that the changing nature of the economy required.

These presidents also sought to "Europeanize" their country. One of them, Domingo Sarmiento, had eloquently expressed this philosophy in *Facundo*, his study of one of the caudillos of the earlier period, subtitled "Civilization and Barbarism." For Sarmiento, Europe and its influences were clearly civilization, and the indigenous American culture was barbarism. One of the various means used to try to "Europeanize" the country was through the extension of public education. Sarmiento himself was a teacher; he and other presidents of the period laid the foundation for what was to be for many decades the best system of public education in Latin America. Another means for "Europeanizing" the country was the encouragement of immigration, principally from Europe. Starting in the 1880s, millions of immigrants, mainly from Italy and Spain but also from Eastern Europe, Germany, and elsewhere, poured into Argentina. Many of these came as temporary workers on the great estancias (estates). Because of the reverse seasons of the Southern and Northern Hemispheres, it was possible to work spring and summer in Argentina and then return home to work on farms in Italy or Spain during the same seasons. Others came to Argentina to stay.

The immigrants to Argentina were faced with conditions that were strikingly different from those facing their counterparts in the United States. By the time they began to arrive in Argentina, the country's rich land had already been divided into great estates, and it was not possible for most of them to set up their own rural homesteads. Thus, the immigrants either worked on the large estates or settled down in the cities where they became petty merchants, artisans, construction workers, and the like. The only part of the country where immigrants were able to establish family-farms was in the northeast, in the province of Santa Fe and others to the north. Even there, however, the immigrant farmers became tenant farmers more often than they became landowners.

The Nature of the Golden Age

By the turn of the century there had emerged in Argentina an economy and society often referred to as the "Golden Age." It was a period of apparently great prosperity, of a rapidly emerging economy, in which a substantial proportion of the population was able to greatly improve their standard of living. Although recent studies have indicated that for many of the immigrants the age was not in fact so golden, it *was* for enough of them for Argentina to continue to attract hundreds of thousands of immigrants who came to "make America," as the popular phrase described it.

The economy that developed after 1860 was based essentially upon the cultivation of grain and the production of meat for export to Europe, particularly to Great Britain. Several factors stimulated this kind of economic development aside from the deliberate policies of successive Argentine governments and the entrepreneurial spirit of the new class of large landowners. By repealing the Corn Laws in 1846, Great Britain made a deliberate decision to concentrate on the production of manufactured goods and to depend on trade to obtain the food products that would no longer be produced at home. Argentina was one of several countries whose economy benefited from the British decision.

Two technological developments were also of great importance to the expansion of the Argentine export economy. The first of these was the invention of barbed wire, which made it possible to fence off part of the pampas and, through careful breeding of the scrawny native cattle with prize animals brought in from Europe, to develop a kind of beast capable of providing the beef (and in Patagonia, the mutton) favored by the English consumers. The second development was the discovery of ways to chill and freeze meat. This made it possible to slaughter cattle and sheep in Argentina and ship the meat across the Atlantic in refrigerated vessels, rather than shipping live cattle, which lost much of their weight in the overseas passage. Thus, by the turn of the century sizable numbers of packinghouses had been established in and around Buenos Aires and Rosario to prepare the meat for shipment to Europe and elsewhere.

Much of the development of the economy in this period was brought about by the introduction of large amounts of foreign capital, principally from Britain, but also from France, Germany, and the United States. Thus, although the Argentine provinces built the first railroads, the job of developing a modern transportation system was soon turned over to British and French investors. The public utilities in the rapidly growing cities were also largely installed by European firms. European and American banks and insurance companies came in to handle those necessities of the burgeoning overseas trade. Even large department stores were established in Buenos Aires and a few other cities by enterprising British merchants.

Thus the pre–World War I Argentine economy was a very dependent one. It hinged on the production of large quantities of a small variety of products for export to foreign, principally European, markets. At the same time, much of the infrastructure of the expanding economy was in the hands of firms that had their head offices in London, Paris, or Chicago, rather than in Buenos Aires or Rosario. However, although the export-oriented economy was very dependent for its prosperity on foreign demand for its goods and on the continuing flow of capital and people from other lands, it laid the groundwork for the development of another, less dependent, kind of economy. The failure of Argentine governments and entrepreneurs to develop this kind of complementary aspect of the economy generated the crisis the country faced by the 1930s and 1940s that prepared the way for Juan Domingo Perón—the man who, in his own way, tried to deal with the crisis.

However, at this time, the large and rapid expansion of exports had as its complement the vast expansion of the country's ability to import. The pounds, francs, and other foreign currencies earned from the sale of meat and grain were spent to import large quantities of manufactured goods. Much of the urban population, in Buenos Aires and other cities, was involved in distributing the goods brought in, largely from Great Britain, to the populace at large. Thus, the growth of exports created a market in Argentina for manufactured goods. Even without encouragement from the government, it became possible for some of this market to be supplied by small domestic manufacturing firms that began to make their appearance during the last decades of the nineteenth century and thereafter. These small industries included textiles and clothing, processed food products, and even metal fabrication.

The Nature of the Argentine Crisis of Development

By the outbreak of World War I, Argentina had gone about as far as it could go in terms of economic development based on the expansion of meat and grain exports. The next logical step in its developmental process was to complement its export trade with the growth of an industrial sector that could produce domestically many, if not most, of the manufactured goods the country was importing. In a word, the next rational stage in the development of the Argentine economy was that of import substitution industrialization.

However, for a generation or more Argentina did not take that step. The governments of the period, when they were not hostile to industrialization, were at best neutral on the subject. They were not willing to foster the growth of an industrial sector. The reasons for this were clear. Until 1916 the government was completely in the hands of political elements allied with the large landowners, whose economic well-being was completely associated with the export trade. Even after the middle-class Radical party came to power in 1916, under the leadership of Hipólito Irigoyen, it had no clear vision of the need for developing the industrial part of the economy, and during the fourteen years that the Radicals were in power, few deliberate steps in that direction were taken. When Hipólito Irigoyen, who had returned to the presidency in 1928, was overthrown on September 6, 1930, the government once again passed into the hands of elements directly dependent upon the large landowning class. Therefore, the governments between 1930 and 1943 had an attitude of frank hostility to industrialization.

The landowners, of course, were quite happy with the kind of economy that Argentina had during this period, as they were its chief beneficiaries. However, not only were the material interests of this class closely associated with the continuation of the export trade as the focus of the Argentine economy, but the landowners were also very closely tied emotionally and culturally to the British, Argentina's best customers. They imitated the manners of the English gentleman class, took to playing polo, and brought into Argentine Spanish such English words as "weekend." They took their holidays in Britain or on the French Riviera, where the Argentine millionaire became almost as famous as his North American counterpart. They became pro-British in international politics and remained so during the two World Wars.

However, opposition to having the government follow

policies fostering industrialization was not confined to the large landowning class. The Socialist party, which during this period was the principal political spokesman for the organized labor movement, was strongly opposed to protective tariffs and other measures to stimulate industry on the grounds that as consumers the workers would be forced by such measures to pay higher prices for the manufactured goods they needed. The Socialists also argued that protectionism was special interest legislation designed to benefit a small group of manufacturers at the expense of the mass of the population. Even the manufacturers themselves were cautious about pushing too hard for protective legislation. The great majority of them were immigrants, who feared that a too vigorous opposition to the free trade policies favored by the dominant landowner elements might endanger their position in Argentina.

The Argentine landowning class, it is clear, had no desire to do anything that might interfere with the export economy which served them so handsomely. They feared that any attempt to foster an industrial sector of the Argentine economy might bring about reprisals from the British, who might seek other sources of meat and grain. Indeed, they saw with some perturbation the expansion of production of those commodities in such parts of the British Empire as Canada, Australia, and New Zealand. Although there was little real ground for such fears until the onslaught of the Great Depression, it must be admitted that they had some validity thereafter. In 1931, the national government of J. Ramsay MacDonald abandoned the free trade policies that had characterized Great Britain since the repeal of the Corn Laws, and began raising a tariff wall. Although that represented no immediate threat to Argentina since the tariffs were mainly on manufactured goods, few if any of which Argentina shipped to Britain, the British Empire Economic Conference that met in Ottawa, Canada, during the following summer did represent a direct threat to the Argentine economy as it then existed.

The Ottawa Conference adopted a system of imperial preferences whereby members of the Empire agreed to trade with one another on preferential terms, charging lower tariffs on goods from within the Empire than were levied on those coming in from countries outside of the Empire. Argentina, although she may have been economically part of the British Empire, did not politically belong to it. Therefore, the Argentine government ran scared throughout the 1930s in the face of the threat represented by the imperial preference system. As a result, the Argentine administrations of that period engaged in prodigies of obeisance to the British. They succeeded in getting a partial exception from the imperial preference system for themselves; however, in return they went far out of their way to give favorable terms to British investors, to assure the British of a completely open market for their manufactured goods in the Argentine market, and to make it clear to them that they had no intention of allowing Argentina to be industrialized.

However, the best-laid plans of the prevailing Argentine governments went considerably awry. During the 1930s industrialization made considerable progress in Argentina, in spite of government policy. The economic circumstances of the time dictated this progress. Argentina was at first badly hit by the Great Depression. Her exports and their prices diminished. As a result, there was a shortage of foreign exchange, and the country could not continue to import the same wide range of manufactured goods as had been its custom. As a result, although the Argentine government took no steps to provide protection for industry, the Great Depression did in spite of the government. The outcome was that a wide variety of industries expanded during those years. New branches of the textile and processed food industries were established, a substantial number of metallurgical plants were set up in the vicinity of Buenos Aires, and firms making goods used in the construction industry proliferated. There was a good deal of import substitution regardless of what the governments of the day might have desired. This considerably cushioned the bad effect of the Great Depression on Argentina.

However, until June 4, 1943, the government of Argentina continued to be hostile to the idea of industrialization. It blindly refused to see that if the country's economy was going to continue to progress, it would have to do so in the direction of developing a large manufacturing sector. Frank recognition of this fact was one of the contributions Juan Domingo Perón made to Argentina.

The Social Problem

There was a socio-political aspect as well as an economic one to the crisis of pre-Perón Argentina. This was the failure of the governments before 1943 to take any significant interest in the problems of the country's expanding working class. As a result of the growth of the export-import economy, there began to develop in the last decades of the nineteenth century a substantial urban working class. Increasing numbers of workers began to be employed in the railroads, ports, the infrastructure of the cities, the construction industry, and small artisan shops. Expanding commerce, banking, the professions, and the government came to employ growing numbers of white collar workers.

As the working class grew in numbers, it also tended to grow in class consciousness. Starting in the 1880s the organized labor movement came into existence. Railroad workers, port employees, ship repairmen, printers, and a variety of other kinds of workers began to establish unions. By 1900 the first central labor organization, the *Federación Obrera Regional Argentina* (FORA—the Argentine Regional Workers' Federation), came into existence, and in the decades that followed, several other such bodies of varying political colors were established. These included the *Unión General de Trabajadores* (the General Union of Laborers), the *Confederación Obrera Regional Argentina* (CORA—the Argentine Regional Workers' Confederation), and two rival organizations each claiming to be the "real" FORA.

Many of those who organized and belonged to the labor movement were immigrants, and there was close contact between the Argentine labor movement and that of Europe, especially of Spain and Italy. The immigrants brought with them the radical political ideas then current in the European countries. Thus, the FORA was anarchosyndicalist, the Unión General de Trabajadores was Socialist, and the CORA tended to use the syndicalist *Confédération général du travail* (General

Confederation of Labor) of France as its model.

In addition to the trade union movement, a workers' political party also developed. In 1896 the *Partido Socialista Argentino* (the Argentine Socialist party) was established under the leadership of a young doctor, Juan B. Justo, who had started his political life as a Radical. The party grew slowly, but by 1904 it had elected its first member of the Chamber of Deputies, the picturesque, mustachioed Alfredo Palacios. Subsequently, the Socialist delegation in both the Chamber and the Senate grew slowly but steadily.

The governments of the time gave little encouragement to the new labor movement. Indeed, the conservative regimes in power before 1916 tended to look upon the labor movement as subversive and to react very strongly against it. Laws were passed permitting the government arbitrarily to deport any foreign-born labor leaders who aroused its fear or indignation. Strikes were frequently broken by the police and even occasionally by the army.

The only president before 1943 who had any marked sympathy at all for the labor movement was Hipólito Irigoyen, who served between 1916 and 1922, and returned for two short years, from 1928 to 1930. When, during and after World War I, there was a series of strikes, he refused to suppress them with the ruthlessness that had characterized some of the previous governments. He even sought to get recalcitrant employers, such as the packinghouses, to recognize their workers' unions—in the packinghouse case, his efforts were defeated more by the fact that the simon-pure anarchists leading the union spurned any intervention by the government in the situation than by the employers' resistance.

Changes in the Labor Movement

During the two decades before the 1943 Revolution, there were important, albeit subtle, changes in the Argentine labor movement. The era of anarchist domination over organized labor was superseded by a period in which the Socialists were the most important group. They controlled some of the largest national unions, such as the two railroad organizations, the

Unión Ferroviaria (Railroad Workers' Union) and *La Fraternidad* (the Brotherhood), and the expanding *Confederación
General de Empleados de Comercio* (the General Confederation of Commericial Employees). After 1930, they were the
predominant element in the most important central labor
organization, the *Confederación General del Trabajo* (CGT—
the General Confederation of Labor). Although representing a
majority of the working class during this period, especially in
Buenos Aires, the Socialist party had a policy of not trying to
manipulate the trade union movement. It had no party
organization specifically designed to develop and carry out
socialist policy in the unions. The lack of discipline over its
members in the labor movement was partly responsible for the
victory of Perón in the 1943 to 1945 period.

In these decades the Socialist party also expanded politically.
During the mid 1920s it elected a substantial number of
members of both houses of Congress; after the 1932 election,
from which the Radical party was banned, its members
constituted the principal element of the Opposition in
Congress. Although the Socialists lost most of their seats
outside of Buenos Aires once the Radicals were again allowed
to participate in elections, the majority of the congressmen
from Buenos Aires and members of the city government
customarily oscillated between the Socialists and the Radicals.

During the interwar years bureaucratization of the large
organizations in the labor movement was taking place as well.
Collective bargaining in the railroad industry, in the large
commercial houses, in the municipalities, and in some other
sectors of the economy became common. Union leaders devoted
most of their time to negotiating and enforcing collective
agreements; consequently, it was necessary to develop a
substantial bureaucracy. Because the principal unions were
stronger than they had been in the earlier decades of the
century, strikes became less frequent than in the past and were
generally economic rather than political in nature—in contrast
to the earlier situation under anarchist influence. The more
successful unions developed a variety of social services for their
members, including health centers and vacation colonies. The
administration of these programs required the use of a

substantial bureaucratic apparatus.

There thus developed during the interwar period a certain separation between the leadership and the rank and file in the larger and more successful unions. The union leaders came to be seen as administrators of activities for the workers, but the rank and file took an increasingly small role in union affairs. Attendance at union meetings declined, and in other ways as well the average union member was less actively involved in what his organization was doing.

This tendency was undoubtedly reinforced by a change in the nature of the working class itself. Whereas before World War I, a majority of the workers in Buenos Aires and a few other cities were immigrants with European ideas of anarchism, socialism, and syndicalism (which they either brought over with them or learned from fellow immigrants after arriving), by 1943 this was no longer the case. Much of the working class was by then made up of second-generation individuals. Another sector of the working-class population consisted of people who had migrated from the interior of Argentina to Buenos Aires and its environs with no previous experience with unions or political activity. The substantial growth of manufacturing during the 1930s was responsible for attracting hundreds of thousands of such internal migrants at a time when there was very little immigration from Europe.

Within the working class the second-generation immigrants and the internal migrants tended to weaken the hold of the Socialists and other traditional labor political groups. The children of immigrants, intent on becoming "Argentinized," tended to reject the ideas imported by their parents from Europe; however, having been brought up in radical homes, they were not entirely opposed to criticism of the status quo. The internal migrants knew little about politics and were not strongly attracted by the existing political groups. They, too, had serious problems adjusting to a new way of life, and were prone to look for an interested politician in the government to help them resolve their problems.

It should be noted, too, that the established union leaders during the interwar period through 1943 made few attempts to organize the new sectors of the working class. Most of the

workers in the new industries that grew up in the 1930s were
still unorganized in 1943. The Communists alone made
considerable effort to reach them, achieving marked success
among the construction workers but organizing only very
feeble unions in other areas (such as the new metal and
chemical industries, and the older packinghouse sector). It was
among these new industrial workers that Juan Perón was to
find his most fanatical and loyal supporters.

Finally, it is important to note that about six months before
the coup of June 4, 1943, the major branch of the labor
movement, the Confederación General del Trabajo, split into
two rival groups, usually referred to as the CGT 1 and the CGT
2. CGT 1 consisted of the two railroad unions and a number of
others and was completely under Socialist leadership; CGT 2
contained all the Communist-controlled unions and some of
the Socialist organizations, including the commercial employees and the municipal workers. The Socialist schism had
come about as the result of a power struggle between the
railroad unions and some groups associated with them on one
hand, and other unions that resented the railroaders' domination of the CGT on the other. The Socialist party, highly
embarrassed at seeing its members aligned on both sides of the
split, tried to bring about a reconciliation, but its efforts failed
and it gave up.

Government Social Policy Before 1943

In the interwar period government policy towards the labor
movement and the problems of the workers was generally one
of neutrality. Although the adminstrations of the period had by
no means the attitude of unmitigated hostility towards
organized labor characteristic of the administrations before
World War I, neither did they give labor any particular
encouragement. The larger or smaller corps of Socialist
legislators who sat in Congress during that period carried on a
continuous fight for social and labor legislation. Indeed, most
of the labor laws passed before the 1943 Revolution were
Socialist initiatives. However, the Socialists, who were always a
minority in Congress (and usually a small one), had little

support from the successive governments, whether they were Radical or Conservative. As a result, very little labor legislation was in fact passed during that time. The only laws passed that affected most kinds of workers were those dealing with workmen's compensation and some modest legislation governing the work of women and children. In addition to those measures, a few groups of workers, notably government employees and railroaders, had sufficient influence to get some laws passed for their particular benefit. These dealt with medical care, retirement and other matters concerning working conditions. No legislation was passed forcing employers to deal with organized workers. Thus the governments of the period neither tried to break the labor movement as regimes had done in earlier times, nor attempted to aid it.

By the early 1940s Argentina was notoriously backward among the Latin American countries in terms of labor and social legislation. In the two preceding decades most of the other countries of the area, particularly the larger ones, had passed extensive labor codes providing systems of social security and extensive regulation of working conditions (so-called "factory legislation"). They also provided legal recognition for labor unions and employers' organizations, and established the means for collective bargaining between them. Argentina had little of this. Therefore, the situation was ripe for the appearance of someone who, by bringing about the enactment of extensive labor laws, could win the support of the workers, both organized and unorganized.

Summary

In the last quarter of the nineteenth century and the first years of the twentieth, Argentina had developed a highly prosperous export-based economy. The export of grains and meat to Europe—especially to Great Britain—had financed the rapid urbanization of the country, particularly in the Buenos Aires area. It had facilitated the absorption of millions of immigrants from Europe and had provided one of the highest general levels of living to be found in Latin America. However, by World War I, the further expansion of grain and meat exports could no longer serve as a source for continuing development. Argentina had reached the point where industrialization was the next logical step if the economy was to continue to expand. Yet the forces that controlled Argentina, both economically and politically, showed no desire to stimulate industrialization; in fact, they were generally hostile to the idea. Nor did the governments of Argentina during the interwar period show any inclination to deal with the problems of the large urban working class created by the export economy and the industrialization that had naturally taken place.

These two problems gave Juan Domingo Perón his chance. He was to be the first person in control of an Argentine government who overtly took the side of the workers, who (at a great price in terms of the autonomy of the labor movement) sought to encourage unionization, and who brought about the enactment of a large body of labor legislation. At the same time, Perón's government, of which he was first an important part and then the dominant figure, was the first to follow a deliberate policy of industrialization. These actions were to be numbered among his positive accomplishments.

TWO

The Young Perón

There is little in the life and career of Juan Domingo Perón before June 4, 1943, that would have predicted his emergence as the most important Argentine political leader of the twentieth century. Coming from relatively modest origins, he chose a career in the army chiefly as a way of getting an education and assuring the possibility of social and economic advancement. His experience in the military was not extraordinary. He rose in rank and responsibilities slowly and regularly, a fact that suggests he was not particularly outstanding. He gave little indication of interest in politics until shortly before the 1943 coup.

Perón's Background and Youth

Juan Domingo Perón was born on October 8, 1895, in the provincial town of Lobo in the province of Buenos Aires, about sixty miles south of the national capital. There are some who claimed that Perón was an illegitimate child, and he is even noted in Wallechinsky and Wallace's *The Book of Lists* as one of the twenty most famous illegitimate children. However, there is little solid evidence that this was the case. Juan Perón was of Italian descent on his father's side. The name Peroni or Perone is fairly common in Italy. One of the most popular beers in the Naples region bears the Peroni label. Juan Perón's great-grandfather is said to have been an Italian senator from the island of Sardinia. His mother is said to have been of partly American Indian descent. (It is interesting to note that Perón

17

never used his matronymic as most Argentines do.)

Juan was the second son of Mario and Juana Perón. His father was an employee of the local court. As infants, Perón and his older brother, Mario, were placed under the care of their great uncle, a Dr. Perón, who may or may not have been a physician.

When Juan was about five years of age, he was taken by his parents to live in the federal territory of Chubut in the cold and forbidding Patagonia region, where Mario had apparently been given a government land grant. However, even though he had become a landowner, Mario Perón soon abandoned his family. Subsequently, Juana Perón, who continued to live in Chubut, married a man whom she employed as a worker on the small estancia. Her older son, Mario, grew up on the family sheep ranch and eventually became a tavern keeper on an isolated highway in Chubut.

When Juan Perón was about ten years of age, his great uncle, Dr. Perón, brought him to the city of Buenos Aires, for the purpose of providing him with a better education. In Chubut his early primary schooling had been of the most rudimentary type. In Buenos Aires he lived with an aunt who was a school teacher. Perón was not an outstanding scholar, but it is clear that he did well enough to be regularly promoted.

At the age of sixteen, Perón was admitted to the national military academy. He perhaps went there as much because this was a good way for a boy of modest means to get a government-paid education, as for any other reason. The military academy had been established several decades earlier by a German military mission, and its faculty still contained a number of German members when Perón was a student there. In later years he was to say that it was during his academy period that he first acquired his good impression of Germany and particularly of the German military. Perón had a very good record in the academy, and in 1915 he graduated as an army second lieutenant.

Perón's Early Military Career

Juan Perón began his active military career at a time when

Argentina was going through an important political change. This was a period in which the armed forces were generally subordinate to and respectful of the civilian government, playing no independent role in politics. So during Perón's first fifteen years of service his career was a strictly professional one.

Perón seems to have been involved in only one event with important political overtones, but even in that the army was acting under the direction of the civilian president, Hipólito Irigoyen. This was in the famous *Semana Trágica* (Tragic Week), in January 1919, when soldiers were called out at a time of serious rioting provoked by the bloody suppression of a strike in an important metal plant in Buenos Aires. Perón was reported to have commanded a subordinate unit of the troops used to curb the rioting.

However, the events of Semana Trágica were the exception that proved the rule; for the most part, Perón's career before 1930 was unspectacular and apolitical. He held a number of more or less routine assignments in garrisons in various parts of the country and for a while he taught at the National Military Academy. He wrote several tracts on military strategy, but had no opportunity to put them into practice. He rose slowly but steadily in rank, having achieved a captaincy by 1928. Perón was virtually unknown outside of the military at this time, and he was probably best known within the armed forces for his participation in various sports activities. Tall, strong, and of an athletic build, he was good at shooting, boxing, and skiing, but excelled particularly in fencing. At one point he was the army's foils champion.

Many years later, Perón told me that it was in this early part of his military career that he first took an interest in social problems. He claimed that he had been impressed frequently by the poor state of many of the conscripts who came into the army each year. He said that he talked with many of them to find out about the conditions under which they had been brought up. He added that, since he had been stationed in various parts of the country during those years, he had had an opportunity to observe the poor working and living conditions of many of the workers of Argentina, and this, too, had made a deep impression upon him.

Perón's First Marriage

In later years, Perón seldom talked about his first marriage. However, in 1928 he was in fact married to a school teacher, Aurelia Tizon, who was known in her family by the pet name of Potota. She was apparently a woman of varied, if modest, talents. She could draw and paint, read English, and reportedly translated some English military textbooks for Perón. His first marital experience was strikingly different from his two later ones. Perón in those years had no political ambitions; there was no question of his using his wife to further any such aspirations, in striking contrast to the situation with Evita and even with Isabel Martinez. In retrospect, members of Aurelia Tizon de Perón's family remembered Perón as having been a loving husband who treated his wife with kindness and was proud of her accomplishments. Relations were also apparently friendly between Perón's first wife and his mother. This was possibly due in part to the fact that the elder Sra. Perón was still living in Chubut, and saw her son and daughter-in-law only occasionally. This apparently very compatible first marriage of Perón was destined to last only a decade. Aurelia Tizon died in 1938, leaving her husband a widower without children.

Perón's Military Career in the 1930s

The 1930s opened with the overthrow of the government of Hipolito Irigoyen by a military-civilian coup, led by General José F. Uriburu. This was the first time since the 1860s that the Argentine armed forces had ousted the government, but it was to be the beginning of an almost ceaseless process of making and unmaking regimes by the military, a process which is still going on. Since 1930, only two elected presidents have fulfilled their constitutional terms of office—General Agustin P. Justo, who served from 1932 to 1938, and General Juan Perón, who completed his first constitutional term from 1946 to 1952, but, of course, was ousted by the armed forces before he had finished his second term.

The Revolution of 1930, however, was not only a military operation. It had the participation and support of most of the civilian political parties which were opposed to the government of President Irigoyen. These included the *Partido Conservador*, the Conservatives (by then called the *Partido Demócrata Nacional*, the National Democrats), who had been out of office since Irigoyen's first electoral victory in 1916; the anti-Irigoyen faction of the Radicals, known as the *Anti-Personalistas*; and a faction of the Socialists known as the *Partido Socialista Independiente*, the Independent Socialist party. In having the participation of important civilian elements, the 1930 Revolution was to be in striking contrast with that of 1943.

The 1930 Revolution was of immense significance for the future of Argentina, and Juan Perón had an active although minor part in it. Still a captain, he is said to have commanded part of the military group that seized control of the presidential palace (the Casa Rosada) and the streets around it on September 6. This was another matter Perón did not talk about in later years. When he began to emerge as an important political figure, particularly interested in gaining support among the organized workers, he sought to associate his name with that of President Irigoyen. By the 1940s Irigoyen was remembered as the only Argentine president who had been friendly towards the organized labor movement. Certainly, the attempt to couple the names of Irigoyen and Perón would have been clouded if great publicity had been given to the role which Perón had played in helping to oust President Irigoyen.

Throughout the rest of the 1930s, Perón continued to rise in the military hierarchy. By 1936 he had reached the rank of lieutenant colonel. That year he was sent to Chile to serve as Argentine military attaché. From this assignment there arose a story that circulated widely and appeared in several books about Perón and Evita. Perón was said to have been caught in an act of espionage, declared persona non grata by the Chilean government, and forced to return home. The story evidently was false. In 1972 I had occasion to discuss the incident in question with Eduardo Alessandri, son of Arturo Alessandri, president of Chile during the period of Perón's service in the Argentine Embassy there, and the son who was politically closest to his father. Eduardo Alessandri absolutely denied that it was Perón who was involved in the espionage incident. On the contrary, Alessandri claimed that during his stay in Chile, Colonel Perón was on very friendly terms with President Alessandri and several of his sons. When the incident occurred, he said, Perón was already back in Argentina, but sent word to the Chilean president that he would never have been so foolish as to do what his successor had done.

The successor, by historic irony, was Colonel Eduardo Lonardi, the man who many years later was also to be Perón's successor as president of Argentina. It was Lonardi, not Perón, who was caught red-handed by Chilean agents while copying secret Chilean military documents, and whose recall was immediately demanded by President Alessandri. Since the incident was not given publicity at the time, it is very difficult to confirm or deny the late Eduardo Alessandri's version of the story. However, there is no question about the fact that Alessandri was in a position to know the truth about the matter, and he had no particular reason to lie to me about it.

Perón's European Experience

Soon after returning from Chile, Colonel Perón was sent in 1938 with several other officers on a tour of duty to study the military organizations of Italy and Germany. Perón's particular assignment was with the alpine ski troops of the Italian army, and his tour of duty in Europe lasted for a little more than two years. This European assignment was of very great importance for the future of Juan Perón. It provided him his first chance to leave South America and to see Europe, and it undoubtedly enlarged his intellectual horizons and world view. It also strengthened his feelings of friendship for the Italian and German armies; he had considerable contact with both armies in those years, and was apparently treated with cordiality and respect by them. It also undoubtedly convinced him that the Axis was going to win World War II, since he was there at the time of the first major victories of the Axis powers. He undoubtedly developed ideas about how Argentina could profit from this expected triumph.

However, the tour of duty in Italy was important for Perón in other ways. It gave him a chance to study in some detail and at first hand the way in which the fascist regime of Benito Mussolini had reorganized, or had tried to reorganize, Italian society. He could observe personally Mussolini's mechanism for mobilizing the masses. Perhaps he also got some insights about the use of flamboyant oratory before great crowds and the theatrical staging of mass meetings. Finally, he may also have found instructive the way in which Mussolini played off the strength of the civilian organizations supporting his regime, the Fascist party and the blackshirt militia, against the regular armed forces to keep himself in power. Years later Perón claimed while talking with me that he had learned from what he thought were the mistakes of Mussolini, and he said that he had had no intention of repeating those mistakes. He argued, among other things, that Mussolini had erred in trying to impose a corporative state structure on Italian society, an attempt which Perón saw as having been a failure.

There is no doubt that Juan Perón's two years in Europe played an important part in his political education. One can only speculate about whether his experience in Italy then aroused in him dreams of being able to do what Mussolini had done, only to do it better. What is clear is that Perón studied carefully the Italian fascist experience. Once Perón was in power, he drew from his understanding of it lessons he had learned of what to do and what not to do.

The GOU

Upon returning to Argentina early in 1941, Colonel Juan Perón was assigned to work with the Argentine ski troops stationed at Mendoza in the Andean area. In March 1942 he was transferred to the Inspectorate of Mountain Troops in Buenos Aires. There he became involved in a very important extra-official activity, participation in the establishment of the *Grupo de Oficiales Unidos* (GOU—Group of United Officers).

In recent years there has been a tendency by some historians of the Perón experience to consider the GOU to be less important that it was seen to be in the years of Perón's rise and early exercise of power. It does seem clear that after the early

months of 1944 the GOU as such came to have relatively little
significance as a group within the new military government.
Thereafter, divisions in the military as well as among the
civilians came to be realigned along a Perón/anti-Perón axis.
However, the GOU was not without importance, particularly
if one is trying to understand the evolution of the Perón
phenomenon. It put forth ideas which were very prevalent in
the armed forces, specifically the army, at the time of the
Revolution of June 4, 1943, and it provided some of the
organizational thrust behind the coup itself.

The GOU was a kind of organization which is by no means
rare in Latin American armies. It was a more or less tightly
organized "brotherhood" or "lodge" within the armed forces,
seeking to commit the military, and perhaps the nation itself,
to a particular point of view. It had its membership among
army officers of the rank of colonel and below. Robert Potash,
who has extensively studied the origins of the GOU, credits
Juan Perón with originally proposing the establishment of the
Grupo de Oficiales Unidos.

Seven officers, including Perón, began promoting the idea of
the establishment of a lodge early in 1942. They won recruits to
the idea principally among staff officers in and near Buenos
Aires. It seems likely that it was not until the formal
establishment of the GOU that they were able to recruit some
officers who had actual command of troops. The founding
meeting of the Grupo de Oficiales Unidos took place in the
Hotel Conte, facing the Plaza de Mayo in Buenos Aires, on
March 10, 1943. A constitution which had been drawn up by
Perón was adopted, and all present swore an oath of secrecy.
They also elected a directorate of twenty officers. These
included three full colonels, thirteen lieutenant colonels, three
majors, and a captain. The last of these was Captain Francisco
Filippi, private secretary to the war minister, General Pedro
Ramirez, obviously a man with a strategic post in the military
hierarchy.

Apparently for the first couple of months of the new lodge's
life, its efforts were concentrated predominantly upon re-
cruiting new members and extending the organization.
However, by May attention shifted to the problem of trying to

prevent President Ramón Castillo from imposing his choice for his successor in elections that were scheduled for September 1943, and which, under the circumstances, were almost universally expected to be rigged.

Castillo himself had reached the presidency as the indirect result of fraudulent elections. In 1938 he had been the candidate for vice president of the political alliance known as the *Concordancia,* consisting of the Conservatives (National Democrats), Anti-Personalista Radicals, and the remnants of the Independent Socialists. This is the coalition that had run the country, together with the armed forces, since the Revolution of 1930 and had maintained itself in power by means of what its participants referred to as "the patriotic fraud." When President Roberto Ortiz, elected in 1938, fell ill three years later, Vice President Castillo took over, first as acting president, and then when Ortiz died in 1942, as president of the Republic. Castillo was widely unpopular. He had governed under a state of siege he proclaimed while only acting president, right after Pearl Harbor. His regime might best be qualified as a semi-dictatorship.

Much plotting was taking place in May 1943. The GOU reached the decision to attempt a coup d'etat in September to prevent the election. War Minister General Pedro Ramirez discussed with a group of Radicals the possibility of becoming the Radical party's candidate in the election, an eventuality that would have made a fraudulent imposition of the president's chosen successor considerably more difficult. However, nothing definite had been decided by the end of the month. The revolution that did take place on June 4 was precipitated by an unforseen development. The GOU played a major role in it in collaboration with other elements of the armed forces, as we shall see in the next chapter.

Before going on to discuss the details of the June 4, 1943, Revolution, however, it is important to take note of a document that was widely circulated about this time within the armed forces, and later among the civilian population. The document was attributed to the Grupo de Oficiales Unidos. Although Professor Potash has concluded that it in fact did not originate with the GOU, from my own conversations with Juan Perón, I would judge that it nonetheless reflected his thinking and that of most of his closest army friends and GOU colleagues at that time. This document was a study of the current Latin American and world situation. Its basic proposition was that the Axis was going to win the war, and as a result, the world would be divided into a number of spheres of influence. The alleged GOU statement went on to argue that in association with the victorious Axis, Argentina was the logical country to dominate South America. The principal rival for this role would be Brazil, and to isolate Brazil, it was Argentina's task to form alliances with all of the countries surrounding her and to force the Brazilians to recognize the hegemony of the Argentine-led group.

Rapid changes in the fortunes of World War II soon made this view of the world obsolete. The Russian victory at Stalingrad followed by the long and bloody retreat of the German armies from their high watermark in the Soviet Union, the Western Allies' victories in North Africa and landings in Western Europe, and the progress of the American island-hopping campaign in the Pacific all tilted the balance against the Axis.

However, the document attributed to the GOU remains of importance as a reflection of the thinking of many of the younger officers who were the force behind the coup of June 4, 1943. It reflects the kind of things that were their major concerns at the time and indicates what probably motivated the participation of many of them in the military's seizure of power. It also indicates how unexpected the twist was that Colonel Juan Perón, a leading figure in the GOU, would soon give to the 1943 Revolution.

Juan Perón on the Eve of His Ascent to Power

No one could have predicted on June 4, 1943, that Juan Perón was about to emerge as a great popular political leader. At forty-seven years of age, he was a man whose whole career had been within the armed forces; he was virtually unknown outside of the military. Perón was physically attractive, tall for an Argentine, and solidly built. He had sleek black hair and a ruddy complexion. Among those who knew him he was regarded as being good-humored, not overly serious, and somewhat boastful although not irritatingly so. It was known that he had been very upset by the death of his wife, and he was not regarded particularly as a womanizer.

At that point, Perón had apparently not given any strong indication of the abilities that were soon to rocket him to a dominant place in national politics. His undoubted oratorical abilities were as yet untried, at least outside of a small circle of military associates. His capacity for intrigue and political maneuver was as yet unproven. His ability to win undying loyalty from some and undying hatred from others was as yet undemonstrated.

In short, Perón appeared to be an early middle-aged army officer of no great distinction. He appeared to be brighter than some, but perhaps not as bright as others. He was completely untried in the civilian arena, and there did not seem to be any reason to believe that he would be especially successful in it.

THREE

Perón's Rise to Power

On June 4, 1943, the day of the military coup that overthrew the government of President Ramón S. Castillo, it seemed highly unlikely that Juan Domingo Perón would emerge three years later as an elected president of the Republic, drawing most of his support from the members of the organized labor movement. First, Perón was only a colonel, and was outranked by many of the officers associated with the coup against Castillo. Second, he was virtually unknown outside the ranks of the armed forces. Third, he apparently had had relatively little contact before the events of June 4, 1943, with the kind of people who were subsequently to become his most loyal supporters.

However, it *was* Perón who emerged from the military dictatorship of 1943 to 1946 as the constitutionally elected president. In the three years that passed between the armed forces coup and his inauguration, Juan Domingo Perón had proven himself a master politician, and had been able to surpass not only all of his fellow officers but also all of the aspiring civilian politicians who might have wished to become president of the Republic.

The June 4 Coup

The military move to take over the government was provoked immediately by President Castillo's attempt to force the resignation of Minister of War General Pedro Ramirez, although it might well have taken place somewhat later in any case. Leaders of the armed forces regarded Castillo's move as absolute confirmation of his intention to impose his choice for a successor and to make the military cooperate with him in the effort.

Several factors made the armed forces' leaders oppose strongly the imposition of Robustiano Patrón Costas as the successor to President Castillo. Perón himself told me that their most important motivation was their extreme dislike for what the military men saw as Patrón Costas' extreme conservatism. There was also certainly strong objection to the idea of being used once more to enforce the choice of a president by fraudulent elections. In addition, no doubt many of the pro-Axis officers, specifically among the colonels and lower ranks, were against Patrón Costas because, as one of the country's largest landowners, he was presumed to be pro-British in the War.

There is no question about the sympathy of Perón and his military associates with the Axis in the early part of World War II. He admitted this sympathy to me, explaining that he and his friends expected that the Axis was going to win the War. In addition, he cited early contacts with German officers in the Argentine Military Academy and noted that during the late 1930s when he and other Argentine officers had been guests of the Italian and German armed forces, they had been treated with respect and friendship. The Argentine officers had participated in maneuvers of the Axis armed forces, and had become very impressed with their professional competence, Perón said. Their natural inclination, therefore, was to support the Germans and Italians in World War II, he argued.

As we have noted in the previous chapter, the GOU had under way by May 1943 a plan for a coup in September in time to prevent the election, although it is doubtful whether the GOU by itself could have engineered an overturn of the government. The threat to the position of General Ramirez, who had the support of virtually all of the rival factions among the military, threw the GOU together with these other groups, and gave a sense of extreme urgency to the situation.

On the morning of June 3 the president ordered the preparation of a decree deposing General Ramirez as war minister. Word of this spread very quickly in the ranks of the officer corps. General Ramirez himself gave his private secretary, a member of the GOU, permission to try to do something about the matter, but said that he would remain neutral. As a result, by that evening, contact had been established among three separate groups: the GOU; a number of generals and admirals (led by the chief of cavalry, General Arturo Rawson), who had had their own conspiracy afoot against Castillo; and the principal officers of the Campo de Mayo garrison just outside Buenos Aires, who also had been talking about the need to remove the president.

Starting at 10 P.M. on the night of June 3, fourteen officers, all colonels and lieutenant colonels, with the exception of General Rawson, met at the Cavalry school at the Campo de Mayo garrison and planned the movement which overthrew President Castillo the next day. Notably absent were Colonel Juan Domingo Perón and his close friend and hierarchical superior, General Edelmiro Farrell. Perón was not seen by the conspirators until late the following day when it was clear that the coup d'etat had been successful. However, he had sent a proclamation explaining the reasons for the movement to the meeting that was unanimously accepted. Most of the time at the meeting was taken up with technical details of the proposed march on Buenos Aires. There apparently was little or no programmatic discussion, and it would appear that there had not even been a firm understanding as to who would succeed Ramón Castillo as president. Some took for granted that it would be General Ramirez, others that it would be General Arturo Rawson, who in fact led the rebellious troops into the capital.

A force of 10,000 men marched on Buenos Aires from Campo de Mayo and Liniers, another suburban garrison. They met little opposition, except at a small naval station where there was some fighting and a number of casualties on both sides. They took the presidential palace with ease, although President Castillo had already fled to a naval craft, from which he disembarked once the victory of the rebellion was clear. On June 4 President Castillo formally submitted his resignation.

The first person to take over the presidency was General

Arturo Rawson. However, within forty-eight hours he was forced out of office by the colonels who had brought about the coup because of disagreements over his cabinet appointments. His place was taken by General Pedro Ramirez.

Perón's Plotting in the Military

The GOU by no means was solely responsible for the coup of June 4, 1943; it was only one of several cooperating groups. And Juan Perón was only one of the leading figures in the GOU, although perhaps the most outstanding of them. Therefore, it was by no means clear that the GOU would win out in the complicated and sometimes bitter maneuvering among the various military factions that began immediately after the seizure of power, or that Colonel Perón would ultimately benefit from this maneuvering.

The GOU did very well in the first apportionment of posts in the new regime. The key ministry of war post was given to General Edelmiro Farrell, who before the coup had been Perón's immediate superior. He was a man without great ability to maneuver or great interest in ideas, and he seemed to have had boundless respect for these characteristics in Perón. General Farrell gave Colonel Perón the second position in the ministry, making him its secretary. A fellow GOU member and close friend of Perón, Lt. Colonel Domingo Mercante, was given the third post, that of *oficial mayor* (sub-secretary). Perhaps most important of all, in the beginning, was the selection of another GOU leader to be head of the Presidential Secretariat.

During the months that followed, the GOU and Perón plotted to get a dominant position in the military government. They sought to place their own people in positions of troop command, and sought to maneuver people who were hostile to them out of military posts that were of strategic importance. During the last months of 1943, the power of the GOU within the military and within the regime grew apace. Early in October, Perón's friend General Farrell became vice president of the Republic, and simultaneously all pro-Allied military men of importance were removed from posts of significance.

The showdown which brought Perón to a dominant position in the regime took place in January and February 1944. At that time, Allied pressure finally convinced President Pedro Ramirez of the necessity formally to break diplomatic relations with the Axis powers. That action provoked a three-sided struggle among those generals and more junior officers who supported Ramirez' move, nationalistic pro-Axis people who were opposed both to Ramirez' action and to the growing influence of Perón, and Perón and his closest associates. Although Perón was willing to go along with the break with the Axis, he succeeded in avoiding any blame for the move.

The result of this crisis was an almost total reorganization of the military government. President Ramirez resigned, and Perón's friend General Edelmiro Farrell took his place. At the same time, Perón himself became vice president and minister of war without relinquishing his post as secretary of labor and social welfare, which he had assumed a few months before. Subsequently, he was to acquire a fourth post, as head of the post-war Council. Thus, this change in the regime marked the emergence of Perón as the most important figure in the military government. He was to maintain this position until early in October 1945.

Perón had arrived at the position of most powerful man in the regime largely through his ability to maneuver in armed service politics. However, he was to consolidate his hold on power—and to be able to retrieve it when it was temporarily taken from him in October 1945—largely because of his ability to organize a very large and powerful constituency among the civilian population. He had begun this process before the crisis of January–February 1944.

Early Policies of the Military Regime

It was some months before the leaders of the military regime completely broke off relations with the civilian politicians, particularly those of the Radical party. However, they had inaugurated policies in those early months that increasingly separated them from the civilian political leaders and civilian public opinion in general. The very ouster of President Castillo assured the hostility of the National Democrats. The dissolution of congress by President Ramirez shortly after taking power disturbed the leaders of all the parties. The quick outlawing of the main pro-Allied propaganda organizations alienated the majority of the population favorable to the Allies. Government "intervention" in the *Unión Industrial Argentina* (the Argentine Industrial Union), the chief organization of the industrialists, and the ouster of its leadership alienated that significant economic group. Similar intervention in some of the country's principal labor organizations, including the two large railroad workers' groups—Unión Ferroviaria and La Fraternidad—together with the outlawing of the faction of the General Confederation of Labor that was dominated by left-wing Socialists and Communists (CGT 2), turned the labor movement thoroughly against the new regime. Finally, the establishment of extensive censorship of the press gained the regime enemies among the country's journalists and newspaper owners.

The consequence was, therefore, that within a very short period of time the new military regime, headed by General Ramirez, had turned virtually all parts of the civilian population against it. Whatever consolation many civilians may have received from seeing President Castillo fall was destroyed by the early actions of the military government. Relations between the regime and the civilian political leaders reached a crisis with the promulgation of three new decree-laws on December 31, 1943. These outlawed all political parties, reestablished Roman Catholic education in the public schools, and established strict press censorship on a more or less permanent basis. However, by that time, Juan Perón had begun to develop his own basis of support among the civilians.

Perón's Overtures to Organized Labor

Perón and his closest associates had soon become worried about the growing alienation of the regime from the civilian population. They feared that the military government would not be able to last long if it did not fairly rapidly gain allies among at least some civilian elements. There is evidence that the Perón group first turned to the industrialists in their search for civilian contacts and allies. They strongly favored the country's rapid industrialization and were quite willing to see the government throw its support behind this. They therefore thought that the industrialists would be natural allies for the military regime.

However, the industrialists did not see things in quite the same light. They tended to look upon the military government as a passing phenomenon that would not be in office for very long. Furthermore, most of them were sympathizers with the Radical party, and they felt that when the military regime fell, the logical group next to come to power would be the Radicals. They as a result saw no point in mortgaging the future of the Radical party through an alliance with a military regime that in all probability would not last very long.

Perón and his friends next turned to the labor movement, which in face of the past seemed a highly unlikely source from which to gain support for the military regime. The Argentine trade union movement, whether led by anarchists, syndicalists, Socialists or Communists, had always had a tradition of strong opposition to militarism and the armed forces. Certainly the early moves of the Ramirez regime had not given them any reason to break with this tradition. However, some of the Perón group had already established contacts of a sort with the organized labor movement. Some of them had served as "interventors" in the various unions that the government had taken over in its early days. The conduct of at least a few of these soldiers in discharging their duties in the particular unions over which they had control had gained at least a little confidence from the workers involved. At least they had established a basis for discussions between the colonels' group and important leaders of the labor movement.

A key member of the Perón group in making these early contacts with labor was Lt. Colonel Domingo Mercante. He was the son of a retired member of La Fraternidad, the union of railroad locomotive personnel. He had worked under Perón in his assignment with the mountain troops in Mendoza and in the Inspectorate of Mountain Troops in Buenos Aires. He was one of the early members of the Grupo de Oficiales Unidos, and after the June 4 coup he was named as Interventor in the Unión Ferroviaria.

Discussions finally were arranged between Perón and his friends and a number of union leaders. The military men sounded out the labor leaders concerning their complaints about previous administrations and the things that the organized labor movement wanted from the government. Many of these things, such as a social security system, various types of labor legislation, and a friendly attitude on the part of the government in individual labor disputes, apparently did not sound unreasonable to the military men. However, the officers were not able to get any kind of firm political commitment from the labor leaders—most of whom were Socialists or syndicalists—in return for promises to have the government move forward in the direction that organized labor wanted. The most that the trade unionists would promise was to show public approval for governmental acts they considered pro-labor, and public condemnation for those they felt to be in opposition to workers' interests.

These discussions formed the background for some of the changes in government policy inaugurated in the last months of 1943, particularly those changes which brought to Juan Domingo Perón a wide civilian backing.

Perón as Secretary of Labor

In November 1943, two new positions with cabinet rank were created: the secretariats of labor and social welfare and of industry and commerce. Their titles were "secretary" rather than "minister" because the Constitution of 1853 provided for only eight Ministers, which it listed, and in the way peculiar to Latin American de facto governments, the Argentine military regime felt that (although it was itself an unconstitutional regime) it did not have the right to establish new ministries until the constitution had been changed.

Juan Perón was named the first secretary of labor and social welfare. He had been director of the Department of Labor for a month. But the new institution he now set out to organize was profoundly different from the department, which had been an organization limited largely to collecting statistics, a somewhat pale copy of the Bureau of Labor Statistics in the United States. The Secretariat, on the other hand, was given a much more ambitious role: to draft and sponsor the enactment of labor and social legislation and to intervene actively in the process of labor relations.

During the next two years Juan Perón made the most of the possibilities presented to him by his new post. His activities in this field included the enactment of a great deal of social legislation, the stimulation of growth of the organized labor movement, and increasing intervention in the process of collective bargaining.

During the 1943 to 1945 period a very large amount of labor and social legislation was enacted by the military government. This included laws extending social security (principally health insurance and retirement benefits) to virtually all parts of the working class, laws concerning paid vacations and holidays, labor inspection, limitation of the employers' right to dismiss workers, and a wide variety of other matters. From being a country notable for the paucity of its labor and social legislation, Argentina was converted into one of the most advanced governments in this respect. Each of these decree-laws bore the name of Perón as secretary of labor and social welfare.

However, Perón's work was by no means confined to seeing that laws were written. He very actively encouraged the organization of the workers of Argentina. He visited the headquarters of the older unions, such as the railroad workers, the telephone workers, and others, encouraging their efforts to bring all of the employees in their jurisdictions into their organizations. Furthermore, even more important was his leadership in breaking down the resistance of employers' groups who for a generation or more had frustrated all efforts of their workers to unionize—and had steadfastly refused to bargain with those that did. Especially in the industrial ring around Buenos Aires, Perón forced employers to recognize and bargain with unions among the packinghouse workers, the metal workers, and in hitherto unorganized parts of the textile industry. Almost completely new unions, with hundreds of thousands of workers apiece were brought into existence with the backing of the secretary of labor, and through him, the military government.

When Perón went out to the town of Berisso, near La Plata, at the height of a packinghouse workers' strike and was seen to confer publicly with the leader of the walkout, Cipriano Reyes, it was no longer possible for the large foreign-owned packinghouses to refuse to negotiate with Reyes and his colleagues. Once and for all, an end was put to the age-old system of labor spies, to dismissals of any workers who joined a union, and to the beating up of labor militants. In its place came a strong union with collective bargaining between union and management.

What was true of the *frigoríficos,* or packinghouses, was also true of the other large industrial enterprises in the metropolitan area. However, Perón's union-fomenting efforts were not confined to the Buenos Aires region. With his help the sugar workers of the northern provinces of Tucuman and Salta were unionized, as were the vineyard and winery workers of Mendoza and other mountain provinces. Even the workers on the great cattle and grain estancias were brought into a union.

Perón did not limit his efforts to encouraging the organization of the workers. To an increasing degree he had his Secretariat intervene in the collective bargaining process itself, generally in a way to force substantial concessions from the employers. Indeed, in particularly important cases it became the custom for Perón himself to preside at the ceremony of signing collective agreements. The workers soon got the impression that Perón intended them to get: it was he who was responsible for the collective agreements and the improvements they brought about, not the union or employee representatives.

Perón developed ways of dramatizing his support of the workers and his association with them. One of the most important of these was the concept of the *"descamisados,"* the "shirtless ones." Although Perón began early to refer to the workers as "descamisados," the word came to be symbolized by his appearing in front of groups of workers in his shirt sleeves. It was a uniform or a suit coat which he—like the workers among whom he was mingling—went without, not a shirt. For many years, therefore, while Perón would appear before a military group in his full uniform, he would appear before a labor group in an open-necked white shirt.

Union Leaders' Reactions to Perón

The great majority of union leaders worked with the secretary of labor during this period. There is no doubt about the fact that they thought they were using Perón to gain advantages for their members, and at least at first they did not see that any issue of political allegiance was involved. Whether they were Socialists, syndicalists, or more or less non-political, they were willing to work with Secretary Perón as long as he was doing things that seemed to be strengthening the labor movement and to be helping them, the labor leaders, to obtain better conditions for their constituents.

However, before long many of these labor leaders suffered a severe shock. They began to discover that it was not they who were using Perón, but he who was using them. They found that their union members were not giving credit to the union leaders for the advances that were being made, but to the secretary of labor, Perón. They discovered that to a greater or lesser degree their ability to continue to keep the support of their rank and file members and to lead their unions had come to depend upon their maintaining a friendly relationship with Colonel Perón. The loyalty of many of the union members had been transferred from the trade union leaders to the secretary of labor.

Of course, there was a minority of trade unionists who resisted the blandishments of Perón. These included the small group of anarchist union officials, virtually all of the Communist labor leaders, and some of the Socialists. With these Perón and the military government were ruthless. Most of the important Communist union leaders were sent to a concentration camp in the far southern part of the country. A number of the anarchists and Socialists were also jailed, and others fled into exile across the Rio de la Plata to Montevideo. If the carrot did not work with the union leaders, Perón was obviously quite willing to use the stick.

Just at the end of his period as secretary of labor, Perón enacted a legal device that had as its basic objective the suppression of those unions that continued to be led by people who refused to become his political allies. This was the Law on Professional Associations. It provided that any union, in order to engage in collective bargaining or to have any dealings with governmental organizations, would first have to have *perso-neria gremial* (official recognition) from the Secretariat of Labor. On the other hand, employers could not refuse to deal with any union that did enjoy such recognition.

Although the terms of this law provided recognition for any union that represented a majority of workers in its category by the Secretariat, in fact the provision was not enforced in the case of unions whose leaders were not Perón's allies. Thus, in the case of the textile workers, neither the Socialist-controlled nor the Communist-dominated union in the field was given recognition, which was extended instead to a totally new organization established by supporters of Perón. Similarly, the *Sindicato Obrero de la Industria del Calzado*, the Shoe Workers' Union, which had had collective bargaining on a national basis since the time of World War I, was refused recognition, and a new *Peronista* union was established and given the right to do the bargaining for all of the shoe workers, although it had only a handful of members at its inception.

By the middle of 1944, the CGT 1 was already controlled by trade unionists who were aligned with Perón. This was demonstrated by the fact that the secretary of labor was invited to be the main speaker at the annual May Day meeting, an invitation extended only after bitter debate within the CGT. During the following year and a half the CGT 1, with Perón's help, became virtually the only central labor organization in the country. (The CGT 2 had already been eliminated, having been outlawed by the military regime soon after it seized power.) The *Unión Sindical Argentina* (USA—Argentine Trade Union), consisting of a group of unions under syndicalist leadership, went out of existence when its most important national unions accepted Secretary Perón's advice to join the CGT. The only surviving rival of the CGT after the dissolution of the USA was the tiny anarchist group, the FORA. There were a few unions that remained independent, namely the new *Federación Gremial del Personal de la Industria de la Carne* (Packinghouse Workers' Federation), a handful of unions under Socialist influence (that withdrew from the CGT when it openly aligned itself with Perón), and a small number of organizations that continued to be under Communist influence. But, by the latter half of 1945 the overwhelming majority of the country's unions belonged to the CGT. It had by that time become the closest political ally of the secretary of labor.

Perón's Growing Power

Colonel Perón's success in acquiring a broad base of support among the civilian population consolidated the power within the military regime that he had originally acquired by adroit maneuvering among his fellow officers. It was clear to all after President Ramirez was succeeded by President Farrell that Vice President Perón was the individual with most influence. There is no indication that President Farrell ever seriously sought to curb Perón's power. The vice president became the chief spokesman for the regime.

It was during the period after February 1944 that the division of the Argentine body politic between supporters and opponents of Perón took place; it was to last for a generation. To an increasing degree, all previous bases of political alignment tended to give way to the issue of Perón/anti-Perón.

Within the military there remained those who were opposed to Perón's influence. The navy in particular was cool towards him, and there were also important figures in the army, politically the dominant arm of the military regime, who were hostile to Colonel Perón. To a considerable degree the issue of where one stood with regard to Perón overshadowed such earlier issues as whether one had belonged to the GOU, or where one stood with regard to the outcome of World War II.

The same was true among the civilian population. Virtually every political party underwent a split on the issue of Perón. The Socialists lost much of their trade union base to him, as did

the Communists to a considerable degree. A leading member of
the inner circle of the Communist party, Rodolfo Puiggros, led
a schism of those who favored working with Perón instead of
opposing him as a "Fascist." An element in the Radical party,
particularly in the province of Buenos Aires, led by ex-deputy
Juan Cooke and Hortensio Quijano, headed a pro-Perón
group, while the bulk of the party's leadership was strongly
against Perón.

The issue of Perón led people to change their lifelong
political habits. Thus, Socialist and syndicalist trade unionists
in whom antipathy for the army had been deeply ingrained
became enthusiastic supporters of a colonel (who was still on
active duty); whereas other Socialist leaders, who shared the
party's traditions of anti-militarism with the trade unionists,
began to conspire with elements of the armed forces who were
opposed to Perón.

Other Policies of the Military Regime

Meanwhile, the military regime of 1943 to 1946 was
developing other lines of action in addition to the Perón-
inspired turn towards organized labor. The government
developed important initiatives in economic policy and in
education. The establishment of the Secretariat of Industry and
Commerce was symptomatic of a fundamental alteration of
government attitude towards industrialization undertaken by
the military regime and later continued under the presidency of
Perón. A basic function of the Secretariat was to stimulate the
development of manufacturing, which was receiving a
substantial stimulus in any case as a result of the protection
from foreign competition which was afforded by the World
War II interruption of traditional trading patterns.

After the 1943 Revolution, Argentina for the first time had a
government which was frankly favorable to industrialization.
The military leaders were motivated in this attitude in major
part by nationalistic and professional considerations. They felt
that economic nationalism was an inherent part of the general
nationalist orientation that was shared by virtually all factions
within the armed forces. More concretely, also, they wanted

Argentina to be able to produce as much of the military equipment it required as possible, and for this to be feasible it was necessary to develop a substantial manufacturing sector, especially in the metallurgical area.

The policies that were to be developed more fully under Perón's presidency, such as making available to manufacturers credit, foreign exchange, and other resources, were started under the de facto government of 1943 to 1946. However, the wartime situation made them less effective than they would be in the years immediately following the end of the conflict.

The military regime brought about another important reversal in what had by then become a traditional policy. At the beginning of 1944 it reintroduced the teaching of Catholicism in the public schools for the first time since the 1880s. Although some of the military men may have believed in this measure as a matter of principle, the main motivation behind it was certainly the desire to obtain the support of the Church for the regime. In this regard it was quite successful, as became obvious at the time of the 1946 election.

In political terms the military government remained exceedingly arbitrary until the last half of 1945, when the defeat of the Axis in World War II made it good policy to relax the severity of their regime. As we have seen, for about a year and a half political parties had been outlawed, censorship had been exceedingly rigorous, and leading political figures had been jailed or forced to flee into exile. However, in response to pressure from the victorious Allies, political prisoners were released, exiles returned, political parties were allowed to function openly once again, and censorship was relaxed. The regime began to promise a return to civilian government through elections, although no specific date for this was named. The United States—for the first time since 1943—sent an ambassador to Buenos Aires in the person of the very activist Spruille Braden.

With the return of some considerable degree of political freedom, the Opposition mobilized. Political parties joined forces to denounce the regime, to call for immediate elections, and to demand the return to constitutional government. This agitation culminated on September 19 when a March for

Constitution and Liberty brought 400,000 people out into the streets of Buenos Aires in protest against the regime.

The government's reaction to this sudden upsurge of opposition was swift. The regime once again granted itself extraordinary powers, and began to round up leading figures of the political Opposition. The press once more was submitted to a considerable degree of censorship. It seemed as if all of the tentative steps that had been taken towards a return to elected civilian government would be reversed.

The Events of October 1945

This conflict between the Opposition and the government dominated by Vice President Juan Perón provided the opportunity for those anti-Perón elements within the armed forces to act. On October 9, 1945, power was seized by General Eduardo Avalos, commander of the major garrison at Campo de Mayo just outside of Buenos Aires. Juan Perón was forced to resign all of his positions and, after being given a chance to make a radio address to his followers, was placed on the prison island, Martín Garcia, in the Rio de la Plata estuary, the traditional place of sequestration of the country's most important political prisoners.

Avalos called upon the political parties to form a new government under President Edelmiro Farrell, whom Avalos allowed to remain in office. However, the party leaders refused to have anything to do with the regime as long as Farrell remained president, and in their turn demanded that General Avalos depose Farrell and turn power over to the Supreme Court, as provided for in the constitution in case of the disappearance of both the president and vice president. This was one of the major errors made by the Opposition in these fateful few days. The Supreme Court had the reputation of being exceedingly conservative and to many workers the parties' demand seemed to amount to putting the government in the hands of a group that would deprive the workers of all of the gains they had made during the previous two and a half years.

Another major mistake was made, this time by many of the

employers. October 12 was one of the paid holidays which Secretary of Labor Perón had established by law. A fair number of employers hastened to put up notices after Perón's downfall that in view of recent events October 12 would not be a paid holiday after all.

Generally, the behavior of the anti-Perón forces in this period played into the hands of Perón and his supporters. They went far to confirm, in the eyes of many if not most of the workers, the claim of Perón that he was their only defender and that without him in power they would suffer severe attacks.

In retrospect at least, it is clear that the political parties should have taken control of the government General Avalos was offering them, should have confirmed the social legislation Perón had enacted (and perhaps added a bit more), and should have invited the CGT and its affiliates to cooperate in the task of returning the country to democratic government. Such action might well have ended the political career of Colonel Perón. There were elements in the Radical party that favored such a policy, but the great majority of the Radical leaders, and virtually all those of the other parties, approved of the refusal to have anything to do with President Farrell.

Perón's followers took the fullest advantage of the errors of the Opposition. In particular, the trade union leaders who had been won over to Perón in the previous period worked to rally his followers against the new regime of General Avalos. A march on Buenos Aires was organized—which brought hundreds of thousands of workers streaming into the city by train, bus, and automobile—to demonstrate their support of the deposed leader. For all practical purposes they took over control of the streets, particularly in the center of the city and in the working class neighborhoods. They demonstrated, they marched, and they beat up some people whom they recognized as being opponents of Perón.

In later years the Peronistas developed the myth that the chief organizer of this march on Buenos Aires was Eva Duarte, then Perón's mistress and shortly to become his wife. However, in reality she had little to do with the whole thing. At that time she was a relatively unknown radio and movie actress who certainly did not have the ability to mobilize the masses in the

way that they were mobilized during the week following
October 9.

If Evita played any significant role in the events of October
1945, it was in connection with Perón himself. She kept in
contact with him when he was on Martín Garcia Island, and it
was reported later that she had argued passionately with him
during this time, trying to convince him that all was not lost,
that he should not accept defeat as he was apparently quite
willing to do. She may well have given him the determination
to struggle to return to power he would not otherwise have
had, but it is clear that her influence on the events of the time
did not go much beyond that.

The reason for the latter-day myth about the role of Evita in
these events is clear. The two men who were actually most
responsible for the mobilization of Perón's trade union
supporters became disillusioned with him and turned against
him shortly after he became president. It was no longer good
Peronismo to give them credit for having saved Juan Perón's
political career in October 1945.

These two men were Cipriano Reyes and Luis Gay. Reyes
was at the time the most popular figure among the
packinghouse workers. Most of the packinghouses were
located within fifty miles of the capital, and Reyes was able to
rally their workers to come into the city to show their support
for the imprisoned Perón. Luis Gay was the head of the
Federación de Trabajadores Telefónicos, the Telephone
Workers' Federation, a former syndicalist who had been won
over to Perón, and who had brought his union into the
Peronista-dominated Confederación General del Trabajo, of
which he became one of the principal leaders. It was these men
who had the contacts and the following required to organize a
major demonstration of force on behalf of Juan Perón. They
did so, and with each passing day the position of the Avalos
regime became weaker.

It is probably true that the military, if their leadership had
been united in the desire, could have suppressed the workers'
demonstrations in favor of Perón. However, to have done so
would have required the spilling of a substantial amount of
blood. Many workers would have had to be shot down, killed or

wounded, in the streets of Buenos Aires. Apparently, the military leaders were not willing to pay this price. A fair proportion of them were still supporters of Perón, and even those who were opposed to him and supported the Avalos regime were not willing to order their troops into the streets to shoot down large numbers of more or less unarmed civilians.

The result was that the move against Perón failed. On the night of October 17 he was brought back from Martín Garcia Island, came to the Casa Rosada, and standing alongside President Farrell on the balcony, told the deliriously cheering crowd of his followers in the Plaza de Mayo below that "I have returned!" He proclaimed that the following day, October 18, would be a national holiday in honor of the fact.

The Significance of October 17

All of these events have come to be known as "October 17." That date came to be, along with June 4, one of the two major Peronista holidays. The events of the previous week, culminating in the return of Peron to power if not to office, were of major importance in the twentieth century history of Argentina. The impact of October 17 is still felt in the country.

October 17 meant the political coming-of-age of the Argentine organized labor movement. The workers had successfully defied the military. They had forced the army and navy leaders who had ousted Perón to back down, to bring him back to power, and to go into oblivion themselves. October 17 meant that the organized labor movement had become one of the two major groups upon which political power would rest in Argentina henceforth.

Juan Perón learned the lesson of October 17 well. He knew full well thereafter that his power rested on maintaining the loyalty of both the organized working class and the leadership of the armed forces. He became adept at playing each of these groups off against the other. He could curb inconvenient demands of his labor supporters by pleading the unwillingness of the military leaders to go along. Even more important, perhaps, he could hold over the military leaders the threat of a new October 17 if they weakened in their loyalty to him. This technique worked for almost a decade, until important defections occurred in both his labor and military camps.

The Election of 1946

Perón did not resume any of his government posts after October 17. Instead, he launched his candidacy for president in an election, the definite date of which was now set for February 24, 1946. He also married Eva Duarte.

For the purposes of the election campaign, Perón had to organize his own political parties since all of the existing ones were aligned against him. The major effort in this field was taken once again by the labor leaders, particularly Luis Gay and Cipriano Reyes. They established the *Partido Laborista* (Labor party), of which Gay became president and Reyes, vice president, for the purpose of mobilizing Perón's labor supporters at the polls. Throughout the country the leadership and rank and file of this group, on a national, provincial and local basis, came principally from trade unionists. Two other pro-Perón parties were established. A small dissident element of the Radical party established the *Unión Cívica Radical Renovada* (the Renovated Radical party) to back him. For the purpose of rounding up the support of anyone who might not be either a trade unionist or a Radical, but might want to vote for Perón, a *Partido Independiente* (Independent party) was also established.

Meanwhile, the Opposition parties had all joined forces to set up what they called the *Unión Democratica* (Democratic Union). The Radical, Socialist, Progressive Democratic, and Communist parties formally belonged to the Unión Democratica and the National Democratic (or Conservative) party threw its backing to the coalition without actually joining it.

The Unión Democratica named joint candidates for president and vice president, but each of the parties in the group ran its own slate of nominees for Congress and lesser offices. The top positions went to two veteran Radical party politicians, José P. Tamborini and Enrique Mosca.

The nature of the campaigns of the two camps was strikingly different. The Unión Democratica candidates talked almost exclusively about political issues, about the need to reestablish political democracy, and they attacked Perón and those behind him as being responsible for the dictatorship of the previous three years. They talked hardly at all about social and economic issues.

Perón, in contrast, talked almost solely about social and economic questions. He pointed with pride to the labor and social legislation for which he had been responsible as secretary of labor. He pictured himself as the paladin of the country's working class. He made promises of additional things that he would do on their behalf if he were elected.

Perón got some considerable help from the government of President Farrell. When the campaign was just getting well under way, Farrell announced the enactment of a new law, attributing inspiration for it to Perón, granting all privately-employed workers a year-end bonus equivalent to one month's wage or salary.

Perón also received some help, albeit inadvertently and unintentionally, from the U.S. government. In the midst of the campaign, Spruille Braden, by then back home and serving as assistant secretary of state for Latin American affairs, had the State Department publish the so-called "Blue Book," which recounted the supposed links of Perón and his fellow officers with the Nazis before and during World War II. Perón, however, turned the Blue Book to his advantage. He denounced it as foreign intervention in the Argentine electoral process, and pictured the voters as having a choice of supporting Perón or supporting Braden. Graffiti "Braden o Perón" continued to decorate walls throughout the country for many months after the election campaign was over.

More intentional was the support that the Catholic Church hierarchy in Argentina gave to Perón's candidacy. It issued a pastoral letter that, without actually naming either presidential candidate or any party specifically, forbade Catholics to vote for any person or group which opposed certain positions supported by the Church. By the process of elimination, the only people for whom Catholics could vote, according to the hierarchy, were Perón and his supporters.

The campaign was a rough one. Both presidential nominees

were shot at upon occasion, although without effect. They were booed and heckled as well as cheered by their audiences. Nominees of both camps travelled widely and long throughout the country.

On election day the armed forces were called out to man the polling places. This was done as much in response to demands of the Opposition as to the desire of Perón and his followers. The function of the military in performing this role was not only to maintain order but also to assure impartiality in the conduct of the election. The actual polling went off with amazing smoothness, given the heightened political tension of the time. Both pro-Perón and Unión Democratica spokesmen praised the behavior of the troops and the election officials, and the heads of virtually all the Opposition parties assured the newspapers right after the polls closed that this had been an exceedingly honest election, and in view of that fact, they were absolutely certain that Unión Democratica had scored a strong victory. It was only after they became aware of the fact that it was Perón and not his opponents who won that many of them suddenly came to the conclusion that the election had been "stolen."

Juan Perón won the presidency by about 54 percent of the vote on February 24, 1946. However, his supporters did much better than that in Congress. They obtained almost a two-thirds majority in the Chamber of Deputies, and subsequently won all but two seats in the Senate—where election was by the provincial legislatures, as had been the case in the United States before 1913.

Juan Perón took the office of president for the first time on June 4, 1946.

Summary

Thus, within three years a relatively obscure colonel, virtually unknown outside the ranks of the military, had won a degree of popularity greater than that of any Argentine political leader since Hipolito Irigoyen, a generation earlier. He had established a powerful, if as yet somewhat disjointed, political machine. He had become the hero and even the idol of an important segment of the working class, while at the same time gaining the undying enmity of large parts of the middle class. He had won a mandate, both in terms of his own vote and that for his supporters in Congress, that gave him a wide degree of latitude in determining what kind of a government he would give Argentina.

FOUR

The First Perón Presidency

When Juan Perón became President of Argentina on June 4, 1946, he had full opportunity to make his regime either democratic or dictatorial. His choice of the second alternative hardened a division among the people of Argentina that already existed, between those who were for Perón almost regardless of what he did, and those who were absolutely against him, virtually without reference to any contributions he may have made to his country's progress. This split made it impossible for over a generation to develop the kind of national consensus that is necessary for a modicum of social and political stability. It bred the kind of suspicion on both sides that made it impossible for either to contemplate allowing the other to come peacefully to power.

Perón's decision in favor of dictatorship clouds his historical record as the leader who came to terms with the crisis in Argentine society that developed between the two world wars. It was largely responsible for the fact that by the time Perón died, his country was facing what was probably the worst situation it had experienced since the days of Juan Manuel de Rosas, one which threatened its very existence as a nation.

Perón came to power under exceptionally favorable circumstances. He had won a free and honest election in which he had received a clear and substantial majority. His partisans controlled almost two-thirds of one house of Congress and all but two seats in the other. He had the secure backing of the armed forces. He had the strong support of the new force which he had brought massively into politics, the organized labor

53

movement. Furthermore, his regime faced a peculiarly
favorable economic situation. The country had acquired large
foreign exchange reserves during World War II. European
agriculture was for the time being in ruins, and the demand
there and elsewhere for the meat and the grain which Argentina
produced was exceedingly strong. The infrastructure of the
Argentine economy was in reasonably good shape, with the
country having Latin America's largest railroad system and a
comparatively new highway system, constructed during the
1930s. Its industries had grown substantially in recent years,
and the prospects for their further expansion, with the help of
Perón's government, were good.

Internationally, too, the position facing the Perón government was highly favorable. The U.S. government, feeling
severely chastened by the failure of the Blue Book's publication
to prevent Perón's election, hastened to send a new ambassador
whose job it was to mend fences with Perón as rapidly as
possible. The British had lost their former ability to coerce
Argentina with threats not to buy her food, which Britain now
needed desperately. The Soviet Union at that point represented
absolutely no threat to Argentina. Even Argentina's great rival
within South America, Brazil, was too busy with its own
internal problems to constitute any threat in the foreseeable
future for its southern neighbor.

It therefore cannot be argued that "objective circumstances"
forced Perón to adopt the road towards a dictatorship. The
choice to do so was taken by Perón more or less deliberately. He
did not want to have his power limited by the framework of a
constitution and the rules of democratic politics. He certainly
had no ideological or emotional commitment to either. He and
his close associates, particularly his wife Evita, were not
willing to undergo strong criticism from the Opposition or to
contemplate the possibility that through losing the strong
majority with which they took office, they might someday
through the power of the vote be forced to relinquish their
control over the country.

The Mounting of the Dictatorship

Several actions during the early months of the new Perón

government gave indications of the direction that the regime was going to take. One of these was the refusal of the Peronista-controlled senate to seat the only two Oppositionists elected to the body. The other was the removal by impeachment of all but one of the members of the Supreme Court by Congress.

By the end of the first six-year term of President Perón's administration, he had drawn the coils of dictatorship tightly around the country. The tendency towards a dictatorial regime had various aspects. These included destruction of freedom of the press, persecution of leaders of the Opposition, gerrymandering and election rigging, expansion of the activities of the secret police, destruction of the autonomy of the labor movement, regimentation of the universities and of education in general, establishment of government-dominated organizations designed to bring virtually all sectors of public life under the control of the State, and a "cult of personality" around Perón and his wife.

During the years following his election, various methods were used to end the freedom of the press. Health inspectors closed the printing plant of the Socialist weekly *La Vanguardia*, and then did the same with any printing plant where the Socialists sought to publish their paper. Eva Perón organized a publishing firm, and through various kinds of blackmail forced owners of a number of newspapers to sell out to her company. The daily newspaper *La Prensa* was taken over through a more sophisticated procedure. The news dealers' union of Buenos Aires presented the paper with a series of demands including such impossible things as giving it control of the sale of the paper's classified ads, one of *La Prensa*'s main sources of revenue. The owners and management of *La Prensa* rejected these demands, the union declared a strike, and the paper closed down for a period. Its own employees backed the paper, but when its management tried to reopen, a mob gathered in front of the building, and in the melee one employee was killed. The government thereupon closed *La Prensa* until further notice. It then "discovered" that the newspaper owed large amounts of back taxes and so seized its property, which it then turned over to the Confederación General del Trabajo. The CGT continued to publish the paper until the fall of Perón.

A kind of footnote to the case of *La Prensa* is that when it was restored to its former owners after Perón's ouster, they refused to recognize that the newspaper published by the CGT had been *La Prensa* at all. They made this clear by numbering the issues of the newspaper from the last one which had been published before the Perón government had closed it down.

Large numbers of smaller papers, especially in the provinces, were closed by another maneuver. Shortly before the beginning of the year 1952, centenary of the death of José de San Martín, the George Washington of Argentina, the government issued a decree that all papers must carry under their masthead the slogan "Year of the Liberator San Martín." But this order was disclosed only to Peronista papers, and scores of small publications that had not been notified were reported to have been closed down on the grounds that they had violated the decree. By the end of Perón's first term, there were no anti-government papers still being published in Argentina. Those publications which were not openly pro-Perón were "neutral." This was the case of *La Nación*, which was *La Prensa*'s rival as the most prestigious newspaper of Buenos Aires.

At the same time that the Perón government was suppressing the opposition press, it was also mounting a persecution of leaders of the Opposition. Many were jailed, such as Juan Antonio Solari, secretary general of the Socialist party, and Cipriano Reyes, who broke with Perón soon after he became president and organized his own opposition party. Others, such as Radical deputy Ernesto Sanmartino and Socialist leader Americo Ghioldi, were driven into exile.

One of the saddest cases was that of Enrique Dickman, one of the most prestigious Socialist leaders. When a member of his family became guilty of corruption in connection with business relations with the Perón government, Dickman was blackmailed: he was threatened that his relative would be jailed for a long period if he did not abandon the Socialists and support the Perón government. Dickman did the government's bidding, a move which ultimately broke his heart.

Another aspect of the development of the Peronista dictatorship was the ending of really free elections. In this, as in the deviousness of the measures to end freedom of the press,

Perón could have been a student of Tammany Hall as well as of the famous dictators of the twentieth century. Some techniques used by the government were to severely gerrymander the congressional districts, to organize large-scale intimidation of the voters, and to arrest Opposition candidates during campaigns (or to forbid any Opposition nominees to run at all). The effects of these methods were clear when in the 1951 election the Opposition was only able to place 14 members in the 150-member Chamber of Deputies.

A major weapon of the Perón government in its attempts to eliminate the Opposition was the development of an extensive political secret police. Most of the expansion of the coercive arm of the government was concentrated on the Federal Police. Until the Perón regime, this had been a body with extremely limited jurisdiction, but after 1946 the Federal Police's area of operations was dramatically increased. It also resorted extensively to the use of coercion and torture in dealing with members or suspected members of the Opposition.

An additional attribute of the emerging Perón dictatorship was its efforts to bring under complete government control all of the important autonomous elements in Argentine society, the most crucial of these being the organized labor movement. Since the task of completely destroying its independence was largely the province of Perón's wife, we shall deal with it in the next chapter on Evita.

The universities were more difficult to deal with than the organized labor movement. From the inception of the military regime in 1943, the six national universities were centers of opposition to the government. Both professors and students protested against the oppressive aspects of the de facto regime, and continued to oppose the Perón government. Perón used various tactics to try to curb the universities. New laws were enacted depriving the institutions of higher learning of the autonomy which they had enjoyed since the end of World War I. The process of purging the faculties that had started under the de facto government was continued by President Perón. However, the students generally continued to oppose the Perón government vociferously. To try to break the students' resistance, the government undertook to establish a rival to the traditional university student organization, the *Federación Universitaria Argentina* (Argentine University Federation). This rival was the *Confederación General Universitaria* (General Confederation of University Students), to which in theory all university students were supposed to belong. However, until the time Perón was overthrown, student resistance remained strong.

The regime also organized a group to encompass most of the country's entrepreneurs. This was the *Confederación General Económica* (CGE—General Economic Confederation), to which in theory all other business organizations—including the Unión Industrial Argentina, the *Sociedad Rural* (Rural Society), the Chambers of Commerce—were supposed to belong. In practice, the CGE became not much more than the organization of pro-Perón industrialists and merchants, falling far short of its goal to regiment all of the country's entrepreneurs by the time Perón fell.

The last of the panoply of government controlled organizations of interest groups was the *Confederación General de Profesionales* (CGP—General Confederation of Professionals). The theory behind the CGP was that all established organizations of members of the liberal professions—lawyers, doctors, dentists, engineers, architects, and others—would become affiliated with the CGP. Here again, the Perón government was still far from having succeeded in its efforts to regiment the country's professional men by the time it fell. For the most part, it was those whose incomes depended more or less directly upon the government—like architects and engineers working for firms with public works contracts, or doctors employed by the social security system—who became members of the CGP.

The important aspect of these government organized and/or sponsored institutions is not the degree to which the Perón regime was able to bring the various interest groups into its ranks and thus under its control. It in fact succeeded more or less completely only with the CGT. The important thing is that the purpose of the establishment of most of these "general confederations" was to destroy the possibility of any significant interest group functioning autonomously without the permission and direction of the government. They were correctly seen by the Opposition and by neutral observers (if there were any) as part of an effort to organize on a permanent basis a dictatorship that, if not totalitarian, would certainly have been highly authoritarian.

The final attribute of the dictatorial evolution of the Perón regime was the development of an exaggerated "cult of personality." The pictures of Perón—and Evita—were seen everywhere. To an increasing degree Perón was cited as the ultimate fount of wisdom on almost any subject one might be discussing or writing about. He was compared—to his advantage—with all of the other heroes of Argentine national history. The cult of the personality was particularly notable in the texts which came to be used throughout the country's public school system. These were full of eulogistic descriptions of one or another of the aspects of Perón and his government's program and contained numerous pictures of him and his wife. Particular emphasis was placed in these volumes on the "New Argentina" which Perón had created.

The Peronista Parties

Perón's direct instruments of political control during his first period in power were the *Partido Peronista* (Peronista party) and the *Partido Peronista Feminino* (Women's Peronista party). They were directly under the control of the president and his wife, and after Evita's death, both were dominated by Perón himself.

The Partido Peronista emerged during the first year of Perón's presidency. He had been elected, as we have noted, as the candidate of three different parties organized for the particular purpose of backing him: the Partido Laborista, the Renovated Radical party, and the Independent party. Of these, the Partido Laborista was by far the most important, winning a majority in both houses of Congress on its own.

After the election the principal trade union leaders laid considerable emphasis on the important role that they and their parties had played in the election of Perón. In all likelihood, one of Perón's motives in ending the separate

existence of the three parties was to attenuate the influence of
the organized labor leaders by merging their party into a
broader one. Another was certainly Perón's fear that controversy might develop among the leaders of the three parties, thus
reducing his control over his followers in Congress and
elsewhere.

In March 1946, several weeks before he was due to take office,
Perón announced that the three parties which had supported
his election would be merged into a single *Partido Unico de la
Revolución Argentina* (Single Party of the Argentine Revolution). He made this announcement without consulting the
leaders of the three parties or obtaining their approval for the
move. There was very little resistance to the merger within the
two smaller parties. Their leaders undoubtedly reasoned that
their influence would be greater as officials of a single pro-
government party than as heads of splinter groups. However,
there was considerable resistance within the Partido Laborista.
This resistance was led by Cipriano Reyes, the packinghouse
workers' leader, who was vice president of the party and a newly
elected member of the Chamber of Deputies. He first succeeded
in rallying a considerable segment of Partido Laborista
legislators against the idea, but after Perón had exerted
sufficient pressure, those remaining as members of the separate
Partido Laborista bloc in the Chamber were reduced to Reyes
himself and one other.

Reyes and his companion continued to constitute a separate
bloc in the Chamber, a part of the Opposition, until the end of
Reyes' term in 1948. At that time, he was arrested on the day his
term ended as he was leaving the Chamber, and was kept in
prison until the end of the Perón regime. In the country as a
whole, the Partido Laborista was reduced to a tiny group.

One of the criticisms made by those opposed to the merger of
the three Peronista parties was with regard to the name chosen
for the new party. It was argued that Partido Unico sounded too
much like a Fascist party. In the immediate wake of the end of
World War II, such an association was not desired by Perón or
most of his followers. As a result, about a year after it was
established the united party was renamed Partido Peronista.

Its companion group, the Partido Peronista Feminino, was

established largely through the efforts of Evita Perón. During the first years of her husband's presidency she conducted a radio program, supporting the government's programs and arguing strongly in favor of women's suffrage, which did not yet exist in Argentina. With the new Peronista Constitution of 1949, votes for women became a reality, and Evita set about to organize the government's female supporters in the new Partido Peronista Feminino, the groundwork for which she had already laid.

From then until the end of the Perón regime, his supporters continued to be organized in the two parallel parties. Members of both were given posts in Congress and other legislative bodies. The Partido Peronista and Partido Peronista Feminino jointly mobilized the president's supporters for mass demonstrations and other occasions.

Justicialismo and Perón's Political Philosophy

Perón needed a political philosophy as well as political parties. There is no doubt about the fact that he considered himself a great deal more than an ordinary Latin American president or dictator. He felt himself to be a figure of hemispheric and even world significance. He not only had a practical program which other countries might wisely follow, he thought, but he had a message which the rest of the world ought to heed. His major problem here was that he really did not know what this message was. On his way to power he had given speeches which laid major emphasis on the predestined role which the military should play with regard to the nation, and subsequently, from time to time, he stressed the preeminent position of the workers in the new Argentina. Military elitism had little popular appeal. There was nothing particularly original about the kind of syndicalist ideas which Perón sometimes used for working-class audiences. He still needed some kind of political philosophy that could be pictured as uniquely his.

President Perón unveiled his supposedly distinctive political philosophy, which he named *Justicialismo*, at a Congress of Philosophy held in Mendoza in April 1949. Then and afterwards, although the ideas of Justicialismo always remained murky, Perón and his supporters pictured them as constituting a "third position," between capitalism and communism, between idealism and materialism, between individualism and collectivism. All of this would seem to tell more what Justicialismo was not than what it was. It remains true that in spite of myriad attempts by Perón, his more philosophically inclined political associates, and others to give firm content to the concept of Justicialismo, they were never able to picture it as a coherent political philosophy. It remained true that Perón's hold on his followers—unlike those of Fascist or Communist leaders—depended almost exclusively upon what he had done for them and promised to do for them in the future, and upon the enemies he had mobilized them to fight, rather than on any attractive set of ideas which he set before them.

Without doubt the reason for this is that Juan Perón never really had any clear political philosophy in which he believed and which he consistently advocated. He was certainly not a convinced democrat, but he did not have any consistent belief in a particular kind of dictatorship. He had no unique world view which presented what he did and thought in some universal context. Over the many years of his activity in Argentine politics, Perón at different times appealed to military elitism, disdain for militarism, working-class syndicalism, social Catholicism, anticlericalism, and various other themes. However, these disparate and sometimes contradictory ideas were never really integrated into a consistent philosophical context. In fact, the only theme which seems to be consistent throughout Perón's political career is that of Argentine nationalism. Although many of his opponents criticized many of his actions as being betrayals of the national interest, Perón defended even these, including his oil policy, in nationalistic terms. There is no real reason to belive that Perón was not a convinced nationalist.

Various factors can explain Perón's confused (or non-existent) political philosophy. His career in the military, coming as it did before his political career, instilled in him a profound conviction of the unique role of the military, which probably explains his early statement about the special role of the leaders of the armed forces. On the other hand, his treatment by the armed forces leaders after 1955 provides ample reason for the kind of extreme disdain for the military in politics that he expressed to me when I talked to him in 1960.

His success in winning support from the organized workers and the importance of organized labor to his administration probably are sufficient explanation for why upon various occasions he endorsed the establishment of a kind of syndicalist society. The fact that most Argentines are at least nominal Catholics and perhaps Perón's own Catholic up-bringing explain why he upon occasion tried to appeal to this element in the national heritage. On the other hand, anticlericalism is almost as deeply ingrained a factor in Argentine politics as the Catholic religion, which undoubtedly tells why Perón in some cases sought to appeal to that tradition, also.

Finally, Perón's experience in Italy and Germany in the pre-World War II period gave him at least some firsthand experience with these two variants of the fascist system. However, the (to him) unexpected defeat of the Fascists in World War II convinced him that he should not in any way associate himself with the fascist philosophy.

Perón therefore sought a philosophy of his own to justify to history and to his living fellow countrymen his right to rule. However, his search was something less than successful.

The Economic Policies of Perón

Aside from the political policies of the Perón regime leading towards dictatorship, the most important aspects of the Perón period in power were the economic policies of his government. These were designed to stimulate the industrialization of the country and to limit the control of foreign interests over the functioning of the economy. The Peronista policies were designed to use the resources of the agricultural and grazing sector to stimulate the growth of other elements of the economy. At the same time, they were directed towards bringing into the control of the Argentine government those elements that had previously been owned by foreigners.

The economic policies of the Perón government have been

severely criticized by its opponents and by foreign economists. However, there is little doubt that in general terms they were justified by the state of Argentine economic development and the world situation at that period. The only objections that one can rationally make are that Perón went too far in the correct direction and that he wasted many of the resources which were mobilized by his government.

The Stimulation of Industrialization

A major element of the economic policy of the Perón government, again, was to draw upon the resources of the agricultural and grazing sectors to effect the expansion of other parts of the country's economy. President Farrell had facilitated this policy shortly before Perón became president by establishing the *Instituto Argentino de Producción e Intercambio* (IAPI—Argentine Institute of Production and Exchange). It was given the function of buying up the country's output of grain and meat and selling it domestically and abroad.

Perón's original justification for the IAPI was that it was designed to avoid being taken advantage of by Argentina's foreign buyers, as he claimed had occurred after World War I. Through having a single seller of Argentina's products, the country would be able to strike the most advantageous deals possible with those abroad who wanted to purchase them. In practice, however, Perón used the IAPI to drain resources from agriculture and grazing for other purposes. These purposes were several. Some of the substantial foreign exchange resources obtained from the sale of meat and grains was made available to industrialists to import machinery and other equipment that they lacked. Some was also used to bring in requirements for such government projects as the gas pipeline that was built from the southern oilfields to the Buenos Aires area and to open new coal mines in the Rio Turbio region.

However, these resources were also used for other less constructive purposes. Much went to acquire material to reequip the Argentine military, a good deal of which was cast-off World War II equipment of dubious value. Another sizable part of the foreign reserves undoubtedly found their way into the private bank accounts in Switzerland and elsewhere of leading figures of the regime, including Perón's first "economic czar," Miguel Miranda, as well as Evita Perón.

In addition to misdirecting and wasting many resources which were transferred from agriculture, the Perón government pushed the resource shift entirely too far. During most of his time in power, Perón had IAPI pay the agriculturalists and grazers prices for their products that were so low that they damaged the rural sector of the economy. Large numbers of rural entrepreneurs, particularly smaller ones, withdrew from agriculture altogether. The amount of land under cultivation was reduced substantially during his period in office. The agriculturalists were not provided the means with which to replace their worn-out equipment. Thus, a major crisis was provoked in Argentine agriculture.

The decline in agriculture was a major factor in the foreign exchange difficulties that Perón faced in the last years of his regime. The situation was intensified by the fact that some of IAPI's income was used for subsidies to keep the prices of meat, bread, and other essential products relatively low in Argentina itself. These low prices worsened the phenomenon that had been developing for a long time—the Argentines themselves were consuming the vast majority of the wheat and meat the rural sector provided.

Nonetheless, although a large part of the IAPI's resources were wasted with regard to the country's economic development, there is no doubt that an important contribution was made to the industrialization of the country by the use of the foreign exchange resources by the IAPI. This was reinforced by the Industrial Bank, which the Perón administration used to make sizable peso loans to manufacturers who found it difficult to get long-term loans from the private banking system. Further encouragement was given to industrialization by the enactment for the first time of a relatively high protective tariff.

During the early years of the Perón regime, most of the industrial advances were made in the field of light manufactured goods and household equipment. Most of the firms in these sectors were privately owned. However, one major area of expansion of heavy industry in these years was railroad equipment. The railroads were acquired by the regime, and thereafter they mounted a substantial capacity to produce their own rolling stock and other requirements.

In the early 1950s the Perón administration undertook a broad program to stimulate the development of heavy industry, to a large degree under government ownership. One major project was the establishment of a new steel plant, under control of the military's Department of Military Equipment, in the Buenos Aires provincial town of San Nicolas. The government received a substantial loan from the U. S. government's Export–Import Bank for this project. Several other heavy-industry projects were set up in and near the city of Córdoba. These included a plant to produce agricultural equipment, mounted by the Italian firm of FIAT and the Argentine government, and a plant for building small airplanes.

The most important project in the Córdoba area was a new automobile plant. This was built by Industrias Kaiser Argentinas, a firm in which the Kaiser Corporation of the United States was in partnership with Jorge Antonio, a somewhat mysterious Argentine entrepreneur who prospered in the last years of the Perón regime. It was widely believed that Jorge Antonio was in fact acting on behalf of Perón himself. The Kaiser firm's contribution to this new industry, aside from management skills, was all of the equipment of a large plant in the vicinity of Detroit which Kaiser had constructed during its ill-fated attempt to break into the U.S. auto industry.

Industrialization was complemented by the expansion of some other parts of the economy. Perón took particular pride in the notable increase in the size of the country's merchant marine for both transatlantic transport and coast and river service. The government airline, Aerolineas Argentinas, was substantially expanded; a gas pipeline was built to bring fuel from the oil fields of the south to the greater Buenos Aires area; and a beginning was made in opening up the substantial coal reserves at Rio Turbio. The first stage in the development of a nuclear energy industry was even initiated.

Repatriation of Foreign Investments

One of the most severely criticized areas of Perón's economic policy was his effort to repatriate foreign investments. His opponents argued that the country's substantial foreign exchange reserves might have been better used for other purposes. However, this policy of Perón must be understood in terms of the situation that existed at that time. The largest quantity of foreign exchange reserves was in British pounds. However, in the immediate postwar years these were frozen, and the British economy was in a serious crisis. It was highly problematical in 1947 to 1949 when and even if Argentina would be able to receive payment in goods for the debts owed to it in pounds.

Perón therefore decided to use some of the country's blocked credits to buy back British investments in Argentina. In the process, he repatriated virtually all of the outstanding government debt in pounds sterling, and bought back the British-owned railroads and a number of less important British investments in the country. He also used some of the credits in France to repatriate French investments as well.

As a result of these measures, virtually all foreign investments except those of U.S. investors—only a few of which were bought out—were transferred to Argentine government ownership. After Argentina was forced to declare war on Germany and Italy as the price of becoming a founding member of the United Nations early in 1945, the Argentine government had taken over all Italian and German investments as "enemy property." They remained under government control for a decade and a half.

Within the context of the time, Perón's move to repatriate the country's foreign investments made eminent good sense. Although the Perón regime may perhaps be criticized for paying too much for some of these investments, especially for the railroads, it can hardly be faulted for using frozen foreign credits, which it seemed at the time would perhaps never be convertible into goods and services, to relieve Argentina of its foreign debt and of the sizable future foreign exchange drain that foreign investments might engender in the form of profit and interest payments.

Social Policies of the Perón Regime

By the time Perón became president, there was not a great deal that Perón could do to expand the country's labor and social legislation. Most of what was done was in the way of elaborating on what Perón had done as secretary of labor. For example, an overall organization was established to try to coordinate the numerous separate social security systems that had been established between 1943 and 1945 for workers in various parts of the economy.

The main area in which new legislation was passed was that of agricultural labor. Three different laws were enacted in this sector. The Law of the Peon provided minimum wages, paid vacations, one day's rest per week, and other benefits for workers who were employed full time on the nation's estancias and farms. Other laws provided for the establishment each year of the working conditions that were to be in effect for casual laborers in agriculture and established minimum conditions for the country's agricultural renters.

However, the economic crisis which characterized the last years of the Perón regime, as well as the regime's drive to destroy the autonomy of the labor movement, brought severe reversals for the workers in the early 1950s. Among other things, real wages fell substantially during the last years of the Perón regime.

One social area in which the Perón government made a considerable change was that of education, particularly on the university level. For the first time the universities were made accessible to virtually any student completing his or her secondary school education. As a result, the university student population increased manyfold during the years of Perón's presidency.

The Perón Constitution

Perón sought to give organic form to the Argentine

revolution for which he saw himself responsible by having a new constitution written. As a result, elections for a constitutional assembly took place late in 1948 and the body met to elaborate a new basic document for the country during the first few months of 1949.

The new constitution made several important political changes. The Constitution of 1853 had provided that the president of the republic could not be immediately reelected. The Perón Constitution eliminated this provision, thus facilitating Perón's reelection late in 1951. Other provisions strengthened the position of the military by submitting civilians to trial by court martial in certain cases and broadened the powers of the government to suspend constitutional guarantees of citizens' rights. The new constitution also granted women the right to vote.

The parts of the new document of which Perón was obviously most proud were those that incorporated the social aspects of the Perón revolution. A special chapter of the constitution set forth "The Rights of the Workers, of the Family, of the Aged and the Right to Education and Culture." Ten specific workers' rights were set forth, including that of freedom of trade union organization. There were also ten specific rights of the aged which were listed, while the State was pledged to extend special help to mothers and children. Under "The Right to Education and Culture," the State was committed to provide free education from primary schools through the university to anyone who wished it.

The 1949 constitution did not survive the overthrow of the Perón government. One of the first acts of President Eduardo Lonardi in September 1955 was to suspend it and to return to the Constitution of 1853. Even when the Peronistas returned to power in the early 1970s they made no attempt to revive the Perón Constitution.

The Foreign Policy of Perón

During his more than nine years in office, Perón paid much attention to foreign policy. His objectives in this area were to have Argentina give leadership to the rest of Latin America and even to give it an important role in the world at large. His major instruments for this were the Argentine economy, the Argentine labor movement, and the supposed philosophy of Justicialismo. As the economy faltered, Perón's foreign policy faltered as well, and his last years in office can be seen as being characterized by a retreat from the foreign policy that he had had during his early years in power.

During his first years in office, Perón sought to play a significant role on the world stage. He sought to become an intermediary in the expanding Cold War. Early in 1947 he sent a message to all existing heads of state offering his services in an effort to bring together the contending forces and to avoid a third world war. This was followed by a letter to all Latin American presidents, urging them to support his mediating efforts. He received little or no response to these overtures.

A few months later, he sent his wife Evita on a trip to Europe, the apparent purpose of which was to impress upon the governments there the importance of Argentina's economy to those countries. She visited Spain, Italy, France, and Great Britain, and even received an audience with the Pope. However, the European reaction to Evita was a mixture of derision for her ostentatious display of wealth and protest against her husband's former friendship with the Nazis. The trip gained little respect or friendship from either the European leaders or the masses.

For a few years, Argentine food was very important to Europe. Perón obviously sought to exploit this fact. However, the situation is perhaps best summed up by the comment an important official of the Spanish government made to me in 1951, when he said that the Franco government had tried to get the best of Perón in their negotiations and Perón had tried to get the best of the Franco regime, and on balance the Spanish official concluded that the Franco government had come out ahead. It had gained Perón's support against the postwar economic boycott of the Allies, had received large quantities of Argentine grain and meat on credit, and had had to pay little for these things.

Thus, Perón failed to develop for himself any role of world leadership. Nevertheless, for a while he was more successful in the more limited area of Latin America. Here, too, Perón counted heavily on the postwar strength of the Argentine economy. His thrust in Latin America was twofold. On the one hand, he sought to form an economic—and hopefully political—bloc with other Latin American countries, particularly those bordering on Argentina. On the other hand, he sought to assume leadership in the sometimes hidden, sometimes open, confrontation of the Latin Americans with the United States. To this end, he offered a series of trade treaties and customs agreements to his neighbors. The most ambitious of these was the proposed accord with Chile, which would have established a common market, would have guaranteed Argentine purchase of substantial quantities of Chile's exports, and would have brought about large scale Argentine investments in Chile. Somewhat similar, if more modest, proposals were put forward to Paraguay and Bolivia.

Although in the beginning there seemed to be considerable enthusiasm both on the part of Argentina and her neighbors for these agreements, in the end they came to almost nothing. Although they were officially accepted by Paraguay and Bolivia, they were never put into execution. In the case of Chile, that nation's Congress finally refused to ratify the agreement.

In an effort to become the Latin American leader against the influence of the United States in the hemisphere, Perón used a variety of instruments. He sought to use the supposed strength of the Argentine economy, as in the Bogotá Inter-American Conference of 1948, where he offered to finance the establishment of an Inter-American Development Bank, a project which most Latin American governments favored, but which the United States did not. The project did not prosper at that conference, and in any case the Argentine economy began to turn sour a year or so later, and its ability to carry out its offers made in Bogotá would have been dubious.

Perón also made use of the Argentine labor movement in his drive against the United States. He established the post of Labor Attaché in most of the Argentine embassies in the hemisphere, and chose most of the occupants of those posts from the Argentine trade union movement. Their job was not only to get to know the local labor movement well, but also to try to win over its leaders to the support of the Perón regime. One method used was to arrange visits to Buenos Aires for labor leaders of the various Latin American countries, during which, among other things, they would be received by Perón and Evita.

When the Argentine CGT was rejected as a member of the new Inter-American Confederation of Workers, established by the American Federation of Labor and many national labor groups in Latin America in January 1948, the Perón government set about to organize its own hemispheric group. This finally took shape as the *Agrupación de Trabajadores Latino Americanos Sindicalizados* (ATLAS—Group of Latin American Unionized Workers), established in November 1952 at a conference held in Mexico City. For a short while, the ATLAS had more or less important labor groups affiliated with it from Nicaragua, Costa Rica, Paraguay, Chile, Uruguay, Colombia, and Venezuela (the puppet labor group organized by the Perez Jimenez dictatorship). However, long before Perón fell from power, the ATLAS had become ineffective.

Perón also made occasional use of the Eva Perón Welfare Foundation in his efforts to win influence in the other Latin American countries. It sometimes made much publicized gifts to groups in various countries at times of natural disasters or when such a gift seemed politically useful.

However, Perón was often his own worst enemy in his dealings with the other Latin American countries. He seemed to be utterly unaware of the deeply ingrained suspicion of Argentina that had traditionally existed in a number of countries, particularly those nearest to Argentina. Thus, he adopted what seemed like an imperious attitude in dealing with them. Quite typical were his dealings with Chile. He openly supported the presidential candidacy of the ex-dictator of that country, General Carlos Ibanez, in the election of 1952. In the wake of Ibanez's victory, there was very widespread sympathy for Perón in Chile. However, he completely dissipated that sympathy when he visited the country for a week, gave patronizing advice to President Ibanez, and interfered openly in quarrels within one of the parties that had backed Ibañez, the Partido Feminino. When he left Chile, there was little sympathy remaining for him and his regime in any level of the population.

By the early 1950s the economic situation of Argentina was beginning to approach a crisis. As a result, Perón needed financial help from the outside. The cost for getting this help, principally from the United States, was that he cease his constant attacks on the United States and its policies. This he did. He had Congress ratify the Inter-American Defense Treaty (the Rio Treaty) of 1947. He received a loan of $125 million from the U.S. Export-Import Bank. As a result of this situation, he was no longer in a position to offer general leadership to the other Latin American countries in presenting their grievances against Uncle Sam. Although his representatives often continued to be critical of the United States in international gatherings, as when they abstained on a resolution of the 1954 Inter-American Conference against the pro-Communist government of President Jacobo Arbenz of Guatemala, the Perón government no longer conducted a consistent campaign of attack on the United States.

On balance, one can say that Perón's foreign policy was a failure. He neither was able to put himself for long at the head of a Latin American bloc in hemispheric affairs, nor (after Europe's economy had recovered) make Argentina's voice heard very much outside of the Americas.

Summary

The policies of Perón during his first presidency had contradictory effects. On the one hand, the economic and social policies of the regime dealt with the two major problems facing the country before 1943. It stimulated the industrialization of the country, including the beginning of the establishment of heavy industry. At the same time, it continued the 1943 to 1945 policy of enacting labor legislation, although there was retrogression in industrial relations because of the destruction of the independence of the labor movement and the decrease in real wages after 1949.

However, what were basically correct economic policies were

carried entirely too far. The process of transferring resources from agriculture to other uses went so far as to undermine the rural sector itself, and many of the things for which these transferred resources were used were counterproductive insofar as the country's economic development was concerned.

Nevertheless, the most serious long-run damage which the Perón administration did to the future of Argentina was in the political field. By installing an increasingly oppressive dictatorship, Perón polarized the Argentine body politic irretrievably between his supporters and his opponents. He generated a distrust that made it impossible for many years to come for Peronistas to allow their opponents to come to power peacefully, or for the anti-Peronistas (once they had control) to permit the Peronistas to come back into office through the electoral process.

The crisis generated by the Perón regime lasts to this day.

FIVE

Evita

María Eva Duarte de Perón, the renowned Evita, was certainly one of the most extraordinary women of the twentieth century. In the late 1970s, a quarter of a century after her death, several full-length biographies, a motion picture about her, and a popular musical record concerning her all attest to the way in which she caught the popular imagination, not only in her native land but in many other parts of the world as well.

Evita remains the subject of great controversy. Among her own countrymen there still exist the most contrasting views of her and her role. These range on the one hand from semi-deification by many of an older generation who were her loyal adherents when she was alive, to attempts to put her somehow in the company of such leaders of twentieth century mass upheaval as Che Guevara, Mao Tse-tung, or Ho Chi Minh; and from grudging respect for her ability and retrospective sympathy for her triumph over material and psychological handicaps, to portrayal of her as the source of unmitigated evil, corruption, and tyranny, on the other. Abroad, too, her personality and her career continue to be the subject of the most divergent interpretations.

Certainly any attempt to assess the significance of Juan Perón in Argentine and American history must take account of the role of Evita. However, in this context, her significance for either good or evil would not seem to be as great as most of her idolators or her detractors claim. One thing is clear. Without Juan Perón, Evita Perón was nothing. She would not have attained the heights of power, popularity, and wealth which

75

she achieved if she had not been his wife. She could not have maintained her position if at any time Juan Perón had decided to deprive her of it. Although Evita Perón was exceedingly useful to her husband, he was absolutely essential to her.

Eva Duarte

Eva Duarte was born (probably in 1919) and grew to adolescence in provincial Buenos Aires. She was almost certainly illegitimate. Her mother supported Evita and her several brothers and sisters first through working as a seamstress and then by keeping a boarding house. During her childhood and adolescence, Eva Duarte undoubtedly experienced not only poverty but also humiliation and contempt at the hands of many of the patrons of the family establishment and many of the townspeople as well.

When she was not quite sixteen she left Junin and went to the city of Buenos Aires to try to make her own way in the world. Her resources for this effort were limited. She had a meager education and little or no training for any particular job. She had few if any contacts in the national capital who could help her get started on a career. Her principal assets were sharp native intelligence, great determination to get ahead, considerable ruthlessness, and undoubted physical beauty, with (naturally) blonde hair, sharp facial features, and a well proportioned figure.

The career she finally chose, or fell into, was that of an actress in the movies and on the radio. In those years the Argentine movie industry was thriving, turning out a wide range of films of all qualities that were shown throughout the Spanish-speaking world. Its stars were world-renowned. However, Eva Duarte never became a movie star. She appeared in some Grade C pictures, and I can testify from having seen one of them that her acting abilities were limited.

Evita apparently received some help in her movie career from the then reigning Argentine cinema queen, Libertad Lamarque. However, Evita felt that the help she received was so patronizing that she was never able to forgive Miss Lamarque for it. Later, when Eva arose to a position of power during the first Perón government, she forced Miss Lamarque to leave the country and to make pictures in Mexico rather than in Argentina.

Eva Duarte also worked on the radio. She gained some following as a soap opera actress. However, in that medium too, her success was exceedingly modest, although the radio experience of this earlier period probably was of considerable use to her after 1945.

One other aspect of her life before 1945 was subsequently the subject of much controversy and gossip. This was her relations with men. In the years when she was the president's wife, it was taken for granted by the Opposition that Evita had been a call girl before establishing her association with Perón. Jokes were prevalent about Evita as *"la gran puta"* (the great whore). One Radical party deputy, annoyed at the encomiums with which his Peronista colleagues were praising Sra. de Perón, had the temerity to proclaim that she was nothing but a whore with whom he had slept long before she became Perón's mistress. He spent the rest of the Perón regime in Montevideo.

Her defenders deny that Eva Duarte had a career as a prostitute (high class or otherwise) while she was working in the movies and on the radio. I have no way of knowing the truth of the matter. The only reason why it is of any significance in trying to assess the role which Eva Duarte played during the years that she was the wife of the president is that the widespread supposition that she had in fact been a prostitute undoubtedly intensified the opposition of the leaders of the Armed Forces to her political role.

However, one thing is certainly clear. This is that, sometime before 1945, Eva Duarte had become Perón's mistress. She kept house for him long before they were married, as her successor Isabel Martinez was to do many years later. She sat in on political discussions and may have contributed to them from time to time. She certainly became a confidante of Perón in his rapidly expanding political career.

It was as his confidante that Eva Duarte served Perón during the perilous days of October 1945. As we have indicated earlier in this book, Evita did not organize the march of the workers on Buenos Aires which culminated in October 17. However, there is good evidence that she did put backbone into Perón, being in contact with him while he was on Martín Garcia Island, and she dissuaded him from giving up and accepting his defeat. It was the iron in her soul, not any popular appeal to the workers or even the trade union leaders (popularity that she did not possess at that time) that helped to save Perón's political career.

Shortly after his return from Martín Garcia Island, Juan Perón finally married Eva Duarte. She helped him modestly during his first presidential election campaign, which followed soon thereafter. However, it was only after Perón's inauguration as president on June 4, 1946, that Eva Duarte de Perón really began her meteoric political career.

The Nature of Evita's Role

Many myths have circulated about the part which Eva Perón played following October 17. As we have noted, it became official doctrine in later years that Evita was herself responsible for October 17. Her admirers have been wont to claim that Eva Duarte was responsible for Perón's own popularity, and that without Evita, Perón would never have been able to gain or remain in the presidency. Her detractors have sometimes claimed that she was the real evil genius of the regime, that most of the more horrendous things done could be attributed to her. The official Peronista myth is that she was a martyr to the Perón regime and to the workers.

The truth, in my opinion, does not lie in these assertions. That Evita was very important to Perón and the regime as long as she had her health is obvious. That she was perhaps even more important in death as a symbol of Peronismo is also indisputable. But, I would argue that her power, either for good or for ill, was nowhere near as great as most of her admirers and many of her detractors maintain.

Evita had one exceedingly severe handicap, one she herself must certainly have recognized. She had at best the critical tolerance and at worst the bitter opposition of the military leaders. In the very male-oriented, macho, double-standard society of Argentina of the late 1940s and early 1950s, the very traditionalist and socially conservative army, navy, and air force leaders were naturally against any woman's playing a leading role in national politics, let alone her becoming their commander-in-chief. Given the tainted reputation—deserved or not—which Eva Duarte de Perón possessed, the resistance of the military leaders was even more determined.

Since the Perón regime rested basically on the twin support of the armed forces and the organized labor movement, the attitude of the military leaders meant that Evita Perón stood no chance of achieving or maintaining power other than that which her husband provided her. Even Perón, at times, had to overlook the slights offered to her by the armed forces and to back down from offering her too much.

It seems clear that Evita herself recognized this situation. The book *La Razón de Mi Vida*, whether actually written by her or not, nonetheless said what she wanted said in her name. If it has any single theme it is that she was nothing without Perón, that "the reason for her life" was to serve Perón. Whatever she might have wished might be the case, she knew very well that in fact that was the situation.

It seems to me that Evita Perón's role during the period from 1946 to 1952 can be divided into five principal parts: first, she was in control of and managed the labor movement; second, she organized and ran a tremendous spoils system; third, she was the eyes and ears of Perón; fourth, she reinforced Perón's popularity with popularity of her own; and fifth, she gave particular attention to the feminine side of the Peronista movement, virtually bringing it into existence, and supervising it thereafter.

Evita's Control over Organized Labor

Soon after Perón became president, his wife established an office in the building of the Secretariat of Labor, which had once been Perón's own stronghold. For about half a decade thereafter, she was for all practical purposes the head of that key department of government. Although during that period José María Freire, former head of the glass workers union, held the titular post of secretary (and after 1949, minister) of labor, it was Evita Perón who in fact ran the ministry and through it the labor movement.

Evita's labor activities were carried out in a variety of ways. It was her custom to hold one day a week free to meet with any labor leaders who had problems that they wanted to bring to her attention. In her wide travels around the country she met frequently with local trade unionists in all parts of the nation. From time to time she intervened directly in particularly pressing labor situations. However, her most fundamental task in the labor field was to bring the trade union movement completely under the control of the government. At the time that her husband became president of the Republic the local and national unions, as well as the CGT, were still largely under the control of the leaders who had headed them before June 4, 1943, the men who had thrown their support to Perón on his rise to power. They were people who had achieved their positions in the labor movement through their own efforts, and who, although often finding after 1943 that their tenure in office depended upon continued loyalty to Perón, nonetheless had autonomous power bases in the labor movement. There always remained the possibility that in times of crisis they might reassert their independence of Perón and the government.

To alter this situation, Eva Perón conducted an almost complete purge of the labor movement leadership between 1946 and 1951. In the Unión Ferroviaria, the Telephone Workers, the *Confederación Obrera Maritima* (the Maritime Workers), La Fraternidad (locomotive engineers and firemen), the Packinghouse Workers, the *Unión de Obreras Municipales* (the Municipal Workers), and a long list of others, the people who headed the organizations at the time of Perón's ascent to power had been replaced by the time of Evita's death. Only in a handful of cases was this purge avoided. Isaias Santin, the leader of the *Unión Tranviaria* (the Trolleycar Workers), was one of the few pre-1943 figures to still remain in charge of his union a decade later. Due largely to his yeoman's work for Perón as minister of the interior, Angel Borlenghi continued through friends to be in charge of the Confederation of Commercial Employees until shortly before the removal of Juan Perón as president. But these were the exceptions that proved the rule.

A variety of methods were used to get rid of the old-time labor leaders. Luis Gay was forced to resign all of his positions—head of the Telephone Workers, secretary general of the CGT, and head of the Postal Savings Bank—early in 1947 as the aftermath of an ill-fated visit to Argentina by a delegation of the American Federation of Labor on Gay's invitation, a visit after which the AFL leaders denounced government control of the Argentine labor movement. The autonomous leaders of the Maritime Workers Confederation were ousted after losing a long-drawn-out general strike (which the government opposed) in 1950. The executive committee of La Fraternidad was ousted by force when a mob attacked the headquarters of the union during a meeting of the committee in 1951, drove out its members, and on the spot "elected" a new executive committee, which was promptly recognized by the Ministry of Labor. In other cases the Central Committee of the CGT "intervened" national unions to remove their leadership—this happening even in the case of the Packinghouse Workers Federation, which was not even affiliated with the CGT.

The CGT itself became a tool of Evita and Perón. Luis Gay was succeeded as secretary general by an old trade unionist, a former Communist, Aurelio Hernandez, who lasted only for a few months. Finally, Evita was able to replace him with a man with the picturesque but appropriate name of José Espejo (Joseph Mirror). His only apparent qualifications for the position as secretary general of the CGT were that he had once been a concierge in a building in which Evita had had an apartment and that he had been active in a union of concierge workers. Espejo retained his job as long as Evita lived.

By the time Evita passed from the scene the Argentine labor movement had been brought completely under the control of the Perón government. Instead of being headed by a group of leaders who had achieved their positions through a career of organizing the workers and bargaining on their behalf with the employers, it was controlled by a group who owed their positions almost completely to the fact that they had been chosen for them by Evita Perón on behalf of her husband. The only exceptions to this rule were on the very lowest level of shop stewards, where more or less free elections were still permitted. However, even there, when stewards adopted too independent an attitude, they were removed by their unions' leadership or by the Ministry of Labor.

There is little doubt that Evita's control of the labor movement was exceedingly useful to Juan Perón. It regimented one of the two main bases of the regime, and assured that the leadership of that power had no illusions that they had any source of power independent of that of the president and his wife.

The Eva Perón Welfare Foundation

The second function of Evita in the Perón government was to organize and manage a patronage system which would have been the envy of Tammany Hall in its palmiest days. However, unlike the management of the labor movement, which would appear to have been a deliberate decision of Perón, Evita's patronage function developed almost by accident.

Before the Perón era there had existed a well-established system of private charity. It was coordinated through the very prestigious *Sociedad de Beneficiencia* (Welfare Society), which was run by the most distinguished dowagers of Buenos Aires society. It had become traditional for the president's wife to be invited to be the honorary president of the Sociedad. However, no such invitation was extended to the wife of President Juan Perón. The lowly social origins and somewhat dubious reputation of Eva Perón disqualified her from this high position in the eyes of the ladies who had it to bestow.

Understandably, Evita was absolutely furious, nor was she one to take this rebuff lightly. Within a short time the Sociedad de Beneficiencia was legally dissolved, and in its place was established a new organization, the Eva Perón Welfare Foundation. The Welfare Foundation was a unique kind of organization. Established by an act of Congress, it was placed completely in the hands of the first lady. She alone was responsible for its finances and its functioning, and by law she was not required to account to anyone for her stewardship of the organization.

The Foundation was financed with exceeding generosity. Aside from periodic appropriations from Congress, it received ample funds from other sources. It became the custom that with the signing of each new collective bargaining agreement anyplace in the country, the first month's increase in wages was "donated" to the Foundation. Businessmen soon learned that they had better give substantial "voluntary" contributions to the Foundation if they wanted to avoid problems with health inspectors, labor inspectors, income tax authorities, or other governmental officials.

The Foundation became a huge patronage machine. It undoubtedly did many good things, such as building housing projects, orphan asylums, schools, hospitals, even shelters for people standing to wait for a bus or a streetcar. But much of its money went to pay for favors that Evita extended to people and to groups on a very personal basis. One afternoon a week, it was the first lady's practice to "hold court" in her office in the Ministry of Labor for anyone who wanted to come to talk with her about any kind of problem which was bothering them. They came to talk about their marital difficulties, their problems with their children, their dissatisfaction with their job, their difficulties with their landlords, anything at all that was on their minds. During these interviews, Evita was flanked by a group of government officials. Frequently she would turn to one or another of them and order that he see to it that a particular person's problem be dealt with. In virtually every case, regardless of what his or her problem was, the petitioner was rewarded with a substantial amount of money, presumably from the treasury of the Eva Perón Welfare Foundation.

As she went around the country, Evita was equally willing to listen to people's problems, to try to resolve them through the government or the Foundation, and, with apparently open-handed generosity, to provide people directly with money. The more substantial projects of the Foundation were also to be found throughout the nation wherever Evita went, wherever she found a need that she thought the Foundation could meet.

However, sometimes Evita's munificence involved giving away property that did not belong to the government or to the Foundation, or even to her. I heard of one of these cases from the mother of one of the people to whom it occurred. A young couple of some means had been planning to be married for some time. In anticipation, they bought a house that was under construction. When this couple returned from their honeymoon, they found that their recently-completed house was already occupied by a family. When they asked about this, they were told that Evita Perón had given the house to its occupants and were told to go to talk to Evita about the matter. As a result, the couple went to one of the weekly audiences of Evita. When they presented their problem to her, she admitted that she had given a needy family the house which the young couple had had built for themselves. When they protested, she suggested that they move in with the young man's family who had plenty of room, adding that they did not need a house all to themselves. Their protests that the house did not belong to Evita and that she had no right to give it to anyone went unheeded by the president's wife. That was the end of the matter, at least until the fall of the Perón regime.

Evita's Wealth

The Welfare Foundation was the most likely source of the very considerable fortune which Eva Perón undoubtedly acquired during the years that she was the president's wife. After her death, some foreign papers speculated that Eva Perón was one of the world's richest women. Whether or not that was the case, the certainty is that she was very well endowed with this world's goods when she died.

Evita was not bashful about flaunting her possessions. She frequently wore very expensive jewelry, rich furs, very costly dresses, and other high-priced raiment. Immediately after the overthrow of Perón, the Lonardi government opened the part of the presidential residence which she had used for the purpose of showing off her vast assortment of clothing, jewelry, and other things that were still there in the hope that workers viewing the collection would begin to have doubts about Evita's supposed concern for the poor and the downtrodden. There were on display hundreds of dresses, hundreds of pairs of shoes, scores of coats and other outer garments, and a large collection of jewelry, much of it very expensive.

Evita apparently saw no contradiction at all between her having exploited her position as Perón's wife to amass very quickly a large fortune, and her public posture as a valiant fighter for the poor and "martyr of labor." She would dress in very expensive clothing even when addressing or visiting working-class groups. She apparently had no worry about the possibility that some of those to whom she was talking might see a contradiction between her words and her deeds.

One of the many stories told about Evita was one about an occasion when she was heckled by someone in a working-class audience who asked her why, if she was such a fighter for the povery stricken workers, she wore such expensive clothes as she had on that occasion. She is supposed to have replied that her clothes were a good illustration of her fight for the workers, because what she was fighting for was that every worker's wife could dress as elegantly and as expensively as she herself did.

Certainly her rapid acquisition of a large fortune illustrates one aspect of her personality. One can suppose that it had some impact in reinforcing the dislike and disdain that the military officer group—and their wives—had for Evita. If the fortune was as large as some rumors claimed, and most of it (as rumor again maintained) was transferred to bank accounts in Europe, Evita's rapid accumulation of wealth may even have had some, albeit modest, adverse effect on the country's balance of payments.

The President's Eyes and Ears

Another aspect of Evita's role in the first Perón government was her function as an informant for her husband. Eva Perón spent much of her time after June 4, 1946, travelling around the country. She conferred with local trade unionists, with leaders of the Partido Peronista Feminino, with rank and file citizens of all kinds. As a result, she had a kind of grass roots relationship with the people of Argentina the president could not possibly maintain.

As a result of Evita's constant contact with the rank and file Peronistas as well as with local leaders of the government parties, trade unions, and other organizations associated with the regime, Evita had immeasurable value to her husband. She could bring to his attention problems that were only just incubating, and of which he would otherwise have had little knowledge. She could warn him of impending crises, tell him of problems before they assumed major importance, keep him aware of the sources of possible discontent among his supporters. In this, Evita Perón's role had striking similarities to that of Eleanor Roosevelt. Both women were able to maintain a degree of contact with ordinary citizens that was impossible for their husbands. Both were able to give their husbands the kind of confidential advice which they could not receive from anyone else.

Evita's Popularity

Together with keeping Perón informed of the thinking and feeling of his followers, Evita Perón added to her husband's popularity. There is no doubt about the fact that Evita Perón mobilized considerable popular support of her own that, given the circumstances of the time, was a reinforcement of her husband's popularity. I shall never forget the old workingman whom I saw staring at one of the innumerable pictures of the late Evita Perón exhibited right after her death, while he wept and mumbled to himself about the tragedy of her death, the blow it meant to the poor people of the country. His number was legion before and after the death of Evita Perón.

There were undoubtedly several reasons for Evita's popularity, aside from her close association with Perón. One was certainly her contrast with previous presidents' wives. No other first lady had ever gone out to the people, mixed with them, talked to them, in the way Evita did. On my first visit to Argentina in 1946 I was struck by the tremendous impression she had made on groups of local trade union leaders with whom she spent considerable amounts of time.

Another factor was her apparently sincere interest in even very humble people with whom she mingled. When she met a group of trade unionists, local officials of the Partido Peronista Feminino, or any other group, she not only talked about the business at hand but she asked them about their families, about their jobs, about other aspects of their lives. She indicated sympathy and concern as well as curiosity. She could be charming and cordial to those whose support she was seeking (just as she could be harsh and vindictive towards those she considered her enemies).

Perhaps another source of Evita's personal popularity was that many humble people saw in her the triumph of someone like themselves. She never tried to hide her own background, she spoke the language of the common people of the country. Pride that one of such an unpromising background as Evita's had gone so far was probably an important ingredient in her popularity with many rank-and-file Argentines.

Evita's Special Role with Argentine Women

Finally, Evita had a special and peculiar role to play in rallying the women of Argentina behind the Perón government. During the first couple of years of the regime, she agitated over the radio, through the press, and otherwise on behalf of suffrage for women and in favor of the rights of her sex in general. Once the Perón Constitution of 1949 had granted women the right to vote, she spent a fair part of her time in organizing and directing the Partido Peronista Feminino, as the women's branch of the Perón movement and government. Her husband left the management of this segment of his followers more or less completely to his wife.

Evita's Mortal Illness

Eva Duarte de Perón died of cancer on July 26, 1952. However, she had been mortally ill for many months before this. This was probably known to her and her husband for at least a year before she died. There is considerable evidence that foreign experts were brought in to try to treat the disease which was ravaging her. Whether or not she knew that she was dying, Eva Perón played out her role as heroine of the Peronista cause to the very end. In retrospect, this is clear with regard to her abortive candidacy for vice president in 1951.

Perón's first six-year term was due to end in 1952. However, for political reasons he advanced the election date by six months. As a result, he had to decide upon a running mate during the last half of 1951. His first choice, apparently, was his wife, Evita. She was officially nominated on August 22, 1951, by the Partido Peronista and the Partido Peronista Feminino to be the candidate for vice president.

However, the military leaders were not willing to accept Eva as vice president and possible successor of her husband as commander-in-chief of the armed forces. They had often shown their disrespect for the first lady. On one occasion, for example, the guards at the Campo de Mayo garrison on the outskirts of Buenos Aires had refused to allow her to enter the camp in spite of her exalted position. Now the military made their opposition clear once again. As a result, a drama was acted out in which, on August 31, nine days after she had been nominated, Evita dramatically rejected the honor, proclaiming her unworthiness to be Perón's running mate and possible successor.

In retrospect, it seems likely that Evita Perón was already aware of the fact that she was the victim of an incurable disease. In any case, it is certain that she died less than a year after she foreswore the highest honor that she had ever been offered. In the months between her "refusal" of the vice presidential nomination and her death she appeared only rarely in public. The last such occasion was the celebration of June 4, the anniversary of the 1943 coup, and one of the two principal Peronista holidays. The ravages of disease were all too evident on Evita at that time, and the myth of her "martyrdom" made giant strides as a result.

The Circus Around Evita's Body

Whatever their earlier relationship may have been, Juan and Evita Perón's union was clearly a marriage of convenience rather than love in its later phases. Each was highly useful to the other, but conjugal love and affection probably had little if any part in their relationship. Nothing made this clearer than the circus which was played out against the background of the corpse of Eva Perón. No man who really had cared for his wife would have used her cadaver for his own political benefit in the way that Juan Perón did.

For many weeks before she died, the inner circle of the Perón regime knew that she was soon going to die, although of course they could not be sure exactly when her demise would occur. Nonetheless, they made extensive preparations for it and for reaping the greatest possible benefit from it for the Peronista cause.

Advance arrangements were made for having her dead body prepared for public exhibition. A provincial undertaker was brought to Buenos Aires and was lodged in a hotel, awaiting the fatal moment. Only minutes after her death, he was already at work preparing her body for the circus. Even so, his work was impeded by zealous Peronistas who watched him ply his trade and were outraged by the "indignities" to which he submitted the body of the president's late wife. Nonetheless, her body was quickly prepared. At the same time, the conditions for exhibiting it in the Ministry of Labor building were arranged. Furthermore, schedules were prepared for every primary and high school class in and around Buenos Aires, as well as the members of virtually every union in the capital and in many of the interior cities and towns, to troop by her casket and pay their last respects to Evita.

Within hours tens of thousands of photographs of the late first lady, complete with a mourning band across the lower left-hand corner, were distributed throughout Buenos Aires and the rest of the nation. In various strategic locations throughout the capital city temporary "memorials" to Evita were built, where her picture was displayed and quotes from *La Razón de Mi Vida* and her other writings were inscribed. There the faithful could pay their last respects to her, even before their chance came to parade before her body.

Meanwhile, national mourning was proclaimed, and it was decreed that only funeral music and tributes to Evita would be played over the country's radio stations for an unspecified period of time. All theaters and movie houses as well as all restaurants serving the general public were closed indefinitely, and goon squads roamed the city assuring that they remained shut. Only foodstores were allowed to remain open and then only for a limited number of hours per day.

Juan Perón played a leading role in this spectacle. He spent virtually all of his waking hours alongside his wife's bier. He was there to be photographed, staring at her body sometimes, gently lifting up old ladies or others of the faithful who from time to time fell prostrate across the glass encased body of his late wife. He was apparently determined to make the most possible out of Evita's obsequies.

The center of Buenos Aires was for many days in the grip of semi-hysteria. Lines of school children, trade unionists, and common citizens stood for many blocks, waiting to get into the Ministry of Labor to see her corpse. Funeral music blared out over the Plaza de Mayo, a block away from the Ministry. People talked in hushed tones. Some stood in front of the innumerable pictures of Evita and wept or mumbled to themselves.

Even the most obdurate opponents of the Perón regime found it hard to escape from this atmosphere of hysteria. An acquaintance of mine, a middle-aged Socialist who hated Perón, Evita, and the whole Peronista movement, confided to me at the time that she purposely avoided going near the central part of the city, afraid that she, too, might begin to weep for Evita.

All of this went on for more than a week. It finally ended with a magnificent funeral. Evita's body was laid to rest in a special tomb that had been prepared in the headquarters of the CGT where it remained until after the fall of Perón, at which time it was spirited out of the country by the newly victorious opponents of Perón and Evita.

Even in the midst of this well-prepared drama there were incidents the ironic humor of which the participants themselves may not have been fully conscious. Soon after Evita's death, some of the country's labor leaders made an official request to the Vatican that she be declared a saint. After a few days they received a reply from the appropriate office of the Holy See in which it was explained that there were many formalities which had to be observed before anyone could be proclaimed a saint—including an investigation and recommendation by officials of the Vatican, proof that the person in question had performed miracles, and had led a blameless life. The message ended with the observation that "This takes years, and sometimes centuries." The irony of this message was probably lost on those who received it.

The Myth of Evita

In death, Evita remained powerful as a myth. Her wealth, her ruthlessness, her vengefulness, were forgotten. She came to be pictured as the indefatigable fighter for the rights of the downtrodden. For some latter-day Peronistas, she was seen as the "true" revolutionary, even after her widower was seen to have abandoned the path of orthodox Peronismo. She was idealized and even deified in the eyes of many who remained loyal to what they thought had been her role in Argentine history.

As long as Perón remained in power, the myth of Evita was propagated by the regime. Texts for the primary schools were rewritten to perpetuate it. One second grade reading text, for instance, had a lesson entitled "Eva Perón," which read:

Creator and first president of the Foundation that bears your name.
Author of the "Rights of the Aged."
Helper of those in need.
For your great works you were declared "Spiritual Chief of the Nation."
Tireless worker on behalf of the needy and the humble.
For your great sacrifices, the people call you "Martyr of Labor."
You died July 26, 1952, the day of national mourning.

Another first grade reader had a lesson showing a child holding a rose up to a picture of Evita, surrounded by a black border, and the following text (in verse):

Evita!
Friend of the poor,
of the aged and children,
Who helps them all,
And brings them your comfort,

what a loving mother,
receive this rose:
that of my love!

But the myth of Evita persisted long after the overthrow of
her widower. It persists to this day. One of those who felt the
weight of this myth most strongly was Evita's successor, Isabel
Martinez de Perón, the unfortunate Isabelita. With Perón's
return to power in the early 1970s and Isabelita as his vice
president, innumerable posters, streamers, and other things
inscribed "Perón-Evita" were seen on the walls and across the
streets of Argentina. Even before Isabel succeeded to the
presidency, there were posters showing her as Perón's helpmate
and colleague, but with Evita's picture hovering behind that of
Isabelita. Inevitably, Perón's third wife, who became his vice
president and successor, suffered from comparison with
Eva, who could not achieve either of these things. One
can only speculate on the part the impossibility of living
up to the myth of her predecessor played in the failure of Isabel
Perón as president.

Summary

Evita Perón's role in the first Peronista government was a
very important one. However, it was not an independent role.
Evita's role was significant for the part she played in reducing
the labor movement to an obedient servant of the regime, in
dealing personally with tens of thousands of humble citizens
for whom the president of the Republic could not spare time, in
keeping her husband informed of what his followers were
thinking and saying, in lending the weight of her personal
popularity to that of her husband.

However, anyone who thinks that Eva Perón could have
stood without her husband is wrong. It was Perón's followers,
people who had been won to his banner between 1943 and 1945,
among whom she worked. She was his helpmate and not much
more. She had little support that was hers independent of her
husband, and she had the strongest of opposition from most of
the military men who backed her husband.

In historical terms, Evita was lucky to die at the height of the power of the Perón regime before its final fatal crisis had fully begun. There is little doubt that during that crisis Perón sadly missed the helping hand of his wife. He might have been spared much foolishness had she still been alive; she might have strengthened his backbone in the crisis' final phases and perhaps the outcome might even have been different. However, then, too, her role would have been one of helping, advising, reinforcing her husband. It would not have been one of independent action.

Dying when she did, it was possible for Evita's myth to persist untarnished. For three years after her death, the full power of the regime was devoted to exalting her image. Subsequently, the myth suffered not at all from the twists and turns of her widower's maneuvering. For loyal Peronistas, whatever errors—and even betrayals—he made, there was always extant the myth of the "true" revolutionary, the "true" Peronista, María Eva Duarte de Perón.

SIX

The Fall of the First Peronista Regime

In at least some ways, the beginning of the end of the first Peronista regime can be dated July 26, 1952, the day Evita died. Although Perón was to remain in power for more than three years afterwards, he seemed to have suffered a kind of moral and emotional breakdown after Evita's death, undoubtedly interfering to a greater or lesser degree with his ability to handle his job as political leader and president. Furthermore, with Evita's death he was forced to undertake supervision of at least some of the things that she had handled on his behalf before her fatal illness. Finally, Perón certainly sorely missed her advice and intelligence gathering in dealing with the growing economic and political crisis he had to face between 1952 and 1955.

Perón's Emotional Crisis

Whether Perón's emotional trauma after Evita's death can be attributed directly to her absence from his life, one cannot say. However, it is difficult to see Eva Perón standing by idly while her husband engaged in the kind of sexual aberrations into which he fell during the last years of his first period in power.

This aspect of Perón's behavior centered around the *Unión de Estudiantes Secondarios* (UES—Union of Secondary School Students). This was one of a series of organizations which the regime was establishing in the early 1950s to mobilize different parts of the population in support of the Peronista government. Among its counterparts were the Confederación General

Economica, established to gain backing among businessmen of
various kinds; the Confederación General de Profesionales, set
up to mobilize the members of the professions; and the
Confederación General Universitaria, organized to try to break
the hold of the Opposition on the country's university students.
Apparently feeling that one way to undermine university
student opposition to the regime was to mobilize and
indoctrinate secondary school students in Peronismo before
they ever got to the institutions of higher education, the regime
established the UES to propagandize, organize, and conduct
social activities among the country's teenage students.

President Perón took a particular interest in the UES. He
apparently found special pleasure in attending their social
affairs, at least some of which after Evita's death were held in
the presidential residence. Much of what was published after
Perón's fall about his behavior at UES parties may have been
exaggerated. However, there is sufficient evidence to believe
that he in fact acted on these occasions with a great deal less
than the dignity of a president of the Republic old enough to be
the grandfather of the youngsters involved. Furthermore, all of
his participation in UES affairs was not just innocent fun. For
at least some time before his removal Perón had one of the UES
girls, a certain Nellie Rivas, as his mistress. Rather torrid—and
in view of the age difference between them, both ludicrous and
sad—correspondence between them was published after his
overthrow.

Perón seems always to have had preference for women
considerably younger than himself. His second and third wives
were several decades his junior. However, the affair with
Nellie Rivas and his general behavior with the UES goes
beyond the bounds of more or less normal sexual preference. It
would seem to indicate that in this period Perón was going
through a middle-age emotional crisis.

The UES incidents may have had their political impact.
Although it is not clear how widely these matters were known
before Perón's fall, one can suppose that they were more or less
widely rumored inside the Perón government. They may well
have contributed to loosening the bonds between Perón and
some of his followers, especially in the ranks of the military

leaders. If so, his relations with the UES helped to undermine his hold on power.

The Purge of Evita's Associates

Evita's death also presented Perón with another kind of political problem. He apparently did not trust the people closest to Evita once she was gone. He therefore felt that he had to remove them from the centers of power and put in their place people of his own choosing. Among those who were removed were the people who had been handling the labor movement under Evita's supervision. José María Freire was soon superseded as minister of labor. José Espejo was also soon removed as secretary general of the Confederación General del Trabajo and relapsed into well-deserved obscurity.

There was also a purge of members of Evita's family. Several of her sisters and their spouses had achieved positions of more or less importance in the Perón regime under the patronage of their famous sister. These rapidly lost their posts. Their brother, Juan Duarte, was even less fortunate. During the last years of Evita's life he had been Perón's secretary. In April 1953 he was officially reported to have committed suicide right after having resigned from his job. Whether correctly or not, it was widely believed, as one leader of the Opposition told me at the time, that Juan Duarte "was suicided."

The Economic Crisis

Meanwhile, Perón was faced with an economic crisis of growing severity. By the early 1950s all of the factors that had worked in his favor a few years earlier and had made it possible for him to appear as the great benefactor of the workers and the militant nationalists had turned against him. By the early 1950s the vast foreign exchange reserves which Argentina had piled up during and immediately after World War II were exhausted. As we have noted, they had been spent to import needed machinery for the country's industrialization, to repatriate foreign investments, and to reequip the Argentine military, as well as undoubtedly substantial amounts that had gone abroad to the private bank accounts of Evita Perón and other insiders of the regime. Furthermore, European agriculture had to a large degree recovered from wartime devastation by the early 1950s. Therefore, the demand for Argentine grazing and agricultural products was no longer as great as it had been a few years earlier, and the prices of the goods Argentina had to sell had fallen substantially. In addition, the impact of Perón's deliberate program of taking resources from agriculture and grazing for the development of other sectors of the national economy had begun to have a quite negative impact on the rural sector. The acreage under cultivation or under use for cattle ranges had declined; at the same time, agricultural productivity had tended to fall because little of the country's foreign exchange resources had been used to replace worn-out agricultural machinery and implements.

All of this was complicated in the early 1950s by several years of disastrous drought. Although Argentina had had droughts at various times in the past, in this case the effects were the most severe that anyone could remember. The country suffered a major agricultural and grazing crisis in the years from 1951 to 1953. Argentina was hard pressed to meet its commitments for the export of grain and meat, and in order to do so was in fact forced to import some grain from places as far-ranging as Rumania and the United States.

There were other additional dimensions to the economic crisis. Many of the firms which the government had taken over after 1943 were run very inefficiently and incurred substantial deficits. These deficits, of course, had to be met from the general government treasury, which was one of several factors that led to an increasingly large government deficit and was a powerful impetus to inflation. At the same time, some of the infrastructure of the economy—particularly the railroads, the highways, and some public utilities—were not maintained adequately, and in these sectors the country was increasingly living off of its capital.

The impact of this crisis was felt strongly within the country. Shortages of meat and pasta, virtually unknown in Argentina before, made their appearance. Meatless days were introduced by government fiat. Some cynical Argentines commented that the government had converted them into canaries, explaining that grain hitherto used to make birdseed was now being used for human consumption. Perón's grandiose plans for economic development were forcibly restrained by the crisis. Because of the growing shortage of foreign exchange, the availability of foreign currency to continue to import machinery for industrial use was sharply curtailed. The crisis was felt, too, in a sharp drop in the standard of living of many of the people. Inflation had been kept reasonably well under control throughout most of the 1940s and, as a result, real wages had been able to rise substantially between 1943 and 1949. Now inflation began to grow at a disastrous rate. As a result, Perón could no longer encourage liberal wages and other concessions to the organized workers, but rather was forced to adopt measures to curb wage increases. The result was that the real wage of the average Argentine worker was probably no higher at the end of Perón's overthrow in 1955 than it had been at the beginning of his rise to power in 1943.

Perón's Response to the Crisis

Perón responded to the crisis in several ways. In the economic field, he partially reversed some of his policies. His political response was to tighten the bonds of tyranny of the regime.

On the one hand, Perón had the Instituto Argentino de Producción e Intercambio raise significantly the prices which it was paying to the farmers and grazers, hoping to stimulate production and discourage the flight from the countryside. On the other, he announced that his Second Five Year Plan, which commenced when he was sworn into office for his second term, was going to put particular emphasis on providing agricultural machinery and other requirements of the rural sector. To dramatize this, he had exhibits organized in Buenos Aires and elsewhere to show the kind of farm machinery that supposedly was going to be provided. Perón also had IAPI reduce somewhat its subsidies of grain and meat products sold inside Argentina.

The government attempted to deal with the inflation by

decree. It established legal maximum prices for a wide range of consumer goods. The press was then mobilized to denounce "price gaugers," and the campaign to keep down prices was dramatized by the closing of a number of stores that were guilty of selling above the legal prices, putting signs on their doors explaining why the places were no longer in business.

All of these measures had at best marginal results. So Perón complemented them with moves to reinforce the coercive aspects of the regime. The autonomy of his supporters in the labor movement was still further reduced. Virtually all freedom of negotiating new collective bargaining agreements disappeared. This was done first by having all collective agreements terminate on the same day, May 1, of each year. Then, the government substituted its own fiat for collective bargaining on the issue of wages. During the last years of the regime, the government announced annually how much of a general wage increase would be permitted.

At the same time, the attempt to regiment virtually all aspects of Argentine society under the aegis of the government was intensified. It was during these years that the various "general confederations" of businessmen, professionals, and university students were established. The efforts, which were of only limited success, at least insofar as the professionals and university students were concerned, sought to destroy the autonomy of all important interest groups in Argentine society.

Meanwhile, political tyranny intensified. The opposition parties were deprived of all but a small handful of their members in the country's elected legislatures. The opposition press was destroyed; in the case of the daily newspaper, *La Prensa*, it was taken over by the government. Hundreds of leading oppositionists were driven into exile or were jailed. A few were forced through torture or blackmail to join the ranks of the government or to adopt a neutral stance towards it.

The secret political police became all pervasive. What this meant is illustrated by two experiences I had in Buenos Aires during this period. The first occurred when I had been talking with an important figure in the Opposition, and we were about to leave his office together. He suggested that we should agree before we left what it was we would say that we had been talking about if we were stopped in the street by the secret police. He explained that the usual police technique was to separate two people, ask each what it was they were discussing, and if the stories did not agree, put them both in jail for an indefinite period. We agreed that we should say we had been talking about the last important soccer game—and he filled me in on a few details of the event. On another occasion I was invited to a meeting at the Casa del Pueblo, the headquarters of the Socialist party. When the meeting broke up and it came time to leave the building, it was agreed that the twenty people present would leave two by two over a period of twenty to twenty-five minutes, since any large group of people seen emerging from that building together stood a very good chance of being rounded up and carted off to the nearest police station.

Retreat From Xenophobic Nationalism

Another response of Perón to the growing economic crisis was to execute a massive turnabout in foreign policy, both in its political and its economic aspects. The beginning of this change came about early in 1953 when Milton Eisenhower, brother of the newly inaugurated president of the United States, visited the country. Until the Eisenhower visit, Perón had been conducting an anti-Yankee campaign that was more violent than that of the Soviet Union at the same time, which was at the height of the Cold War. Perón personally used every opportunity to verbally attack the United States; his press was unremitting in attacking virtually all aspects of U.S. polity and society.

However, the reaction to Milton Eisenhower's visit bordered on the miraculous. From one day to the next, the tone of the Argentine press completely changed. Perón began expressing his solidarity with Western civilization as epitomized by the United States, and even such pet objects of attack as Serafino Romualdi, the Latin American representative of the American Federation of Labor, were apparently forgotten by Argentine labor leaders, publicists, and other spokesmen.

This end to Perón's own Cold War against the United States

soon was reflected in a change in economic policy. A large loan was soon negotiated with the U.S. government's Export-Import Bank and foreign investors were once again welcomed back into Argentina. The result of this was that before Perón fell the FIAT company had established a tractor plant in Córdoba, and the Kaiser Company was in the process of constructing what was then Latin America's largest auto assembly plant in the same city.

Most striking was the abandonment of the nationalistic petroleum policy which had been an article of faith with virtually all Argentines for at least a quarter of a century. The country was faced with a growing deficit in petroleum production, as a result of which increasing amounts of foreign exchange were being required to import the product. Perón apparently became convinced that the government firm, *Yacimientos Petroliferos Fiscales* (YPF—Government Petroleum Enterprise), which had a monopoly on exploration and exploitation of oil within the national frontiers, would never be able to make good this growing deficit without help from abroad. However, having made up his mind on that point, Perón went to extremes in the direction of encouraging foreign firms to help exploit the country's substantial petroleum reserves. In 1954 he signed an agreement with the Standard Oil Company of California that aroused a storm of protest among the Argentine citizenry and gasps of amazement among oil experts in other countries.

The agreement with Standard Oil of California not only gave the firm very extensive concessions in the southern part of the country, but also gave it conditions such as the international oil firms had not enjoyed for perhaps as long as a generation. According to the agreement, most of Argentina's labor legislation would not apply to the operations of the firm; the company would be able to maintain its own police force to keep order 'within the area, thus almost removing it from Argentine sovereignty. In addition, the financial terms of the agreement were much more favorable than those then in vogue among the international oil companies.

This agreement was seen by many, if not most Argentines, as a rank betrayal of Perón's claims to be a strong nationalist. The depth of the opposition to the arrangement is seen in the fact that even the Argentine Congress, usually so willing to do Perón's bidding, for many months did not get around to giving the necessary authorization for the accord with Standard Oil of California, in fact did not do so before the Perón regime was overthrown. His successor let the agreement lapse. There is little doubt about the fact that the proposed agreement with Standard Oil of California seriously weakened Perón's grip on power. It outraged Argentine nationalist sentiment, notably in the ranks of the military. It was undoubtedly an important weight in the growing balance against Perón in the minds of the leaders of the country's armed forces.

On Perón's behalf, however, it should be noted that he was apparently really convinced of the need to bring foreign firms into the process of exploiting Argentine oil resources. In spite of the rebuff in this case, Perón, even after being driven into exile, continued to argue that YPF was not capable of providing the country with the oil its economy demanded, and continued to argue in favor of arrangements with foreign oil companies. There were few issues upon which Perón demonstrated such deep conviction over such a long period of time.

The Quarrel with the Catholic Church

One of the more mysterious aspects of the last years of the first Perón regime was the sudden flareup of a quarrel with the Catholic Church. No adequate explanation has been offered for this series of events, and one can only speculate on their origin.

In conversation with me, Perón denied that he personally had ever had a quarrel with the Church, saying that it had been some of his supporters who had become worried about the growing attempts by Catholic elements to penetrate the labor movement and by the emergence (albeit underground) of a *Partido Demócrata Cristiano* (Christian Democractic party); it was they, not he, who had taken action against the Church. This seems an unlikely version of the events; his followers would hardly have moved without his approval, and much of what was done, was done by the Perón government itself. Perón's name is on the legislation which constitutes part of this struggle, and his speeches constituted another aspect of it.

As we have noted, in the early Perón years the Church hierarchy had had a more or less benevolent attitude towards first the military regime and then Perón's own government. Although relations had cooled substantially by 1951, at the time of a world Eucharistic Congress in Rosario they did not by any means seem to be near a breaking point.

However, during the last year of the Perón regime there was virtually open warfare between Church and state in Argentina. Some reflections of this were the arrest of many priests, the repeal of the decree-law enacted at the end of 1943 by the military government providing for Catholic religious teaching in the public schools, the enactment of an easy divorce law, and the legalization of prostitution. All of these measures were bitterly opposed by the Church, and were strongly supported by Perón. But matters went beyond mere changes in the law. On June 15, 1955, after Perón had delivered a fiery speech from the balcony of the Casa Rosada, his followers swarmed through the center of Buenos Aires, and put the torch not only to such buildings as the Socialists' Casa del Pueblo, the headquarters of the Radical party, and the Jockey Club, but to seven churches as well. On the same day, two bishops were arrested and were deported to Italy.

This deportation gave rise to one of the more confusing aspects of the quarrel between Perón and the Church. The Vatican's answer, as announced in *Osservatore Romano*, was the "automatic" excommunication of "those responsible" for the exiling of the two clergymen. Perón always maintained that he was not one of those who was excommunicated, claiming to have had nothing to do with the matter. However, a subsequent measure withdrawing his excommunication would seem to argue against his interpretation of the event.

Certainly, Perón was personally involved in the feud with the Church. Early in June 1955 he gave a speech in which, among other things, he accused the Church of being "a wolf in sheep's clothing," and adding that his twelve years' effort to maintain friendship with the Church had failed, and that the fault lay with the Church. As a result, this vendetta with the Church (in which the initiative clearly was with the Perón government) undoubtedly contributed to the weakening of the power of the president. On the one hand, the military leadership tended to be generally more Catholic than the populace as a whole; thus many of the officers would be perturbed (if not resentful) at this conflict with the Argentine hierarchy and the Vatican. On the other, a very loyal Peronista among the workers was much more likely than an anti-Peronista to be a practicing Roman Catholic; thus the conflict with the Church in all likelihood sowed confusion and divided loyalties among Perón's civilian supporters.

The Factors Undermining the Perón Regime

It is thus clear that there were many things that were weakening the Perón regime in the years just preceding its culminating crises of June and September 1955. The absence of Evita, to maintain daily contacts with the people and to keep Perón informed of what they were thinking and feeling, was certainly one of these. The growing economic crisis that resulted in a reversal of the trend towards higher real wages (to the earlier lower standard of living) and the slowing down of economic development, was another. So, too, was the sudden apparent reversal of the economic nationalism that had characterized the early years of the regime.

Meanwhile, the intensification of the tyrannical aspects of the Perón government undoubtedly hardened the Opposition and made more difficult any attempt to reach an understanding with it. Finally, the sudden outbreak of a bitter feud with the Roman Catholic Church undoubtedly helped to weaken the loyalties of both Perón's military and civilian adherents.

All of these factors had serious impacts on the stability of the Perón regime. On the one hand, they strengthened those elements in the military who wanted to get rid of Perón. On the other, they undermined his support among the Argentine workers, the other basis of his regime, a fact that was clearly evident when the final crisis came and the workers reacted hardly at all to the ouster of *El Líder* (The Leader).

The First Coup Attempt and Its Aftermath

The first of two attempts during 1955 by elements of the armed forces to overthrow the Perón regime took place on June 16. This was an effort by elements of the navy and the air force, with apparently very little support from the army. Aircraft bombed and shot at the presidential palace from a low altitude. However, after a few hours the revolt was put down and the regime seemed once again more or less secure.

Subsequent to this abortive uprising there circulated various stories about Perón's behavior during the attack. Generally, they tended to picture him as having lost his nerve and as giving little or no leadership to the moves to suppress the insurrection. Whether or not these stories were true, they certainly damaged him politically. *"Machismo,"* or manliness, was still highly prized in Argentina, one of the last countries to give up the custom of duelling, and the widespread belief that Perón had proven a physical coward during the June uprising certainly tended to generate contempt among his opponents, and perhaps even among some of his supporters.

There seems little doubt that this first insurrection frightened Perón politically, even if not physically. His subsequent reactions indicated confusion and an attempt to buy peace. They also gave some indication that he was losing control of the situation. On the one hand, Perón greatly strengthened the authority of the military leaders, particularly those of the army. Extraordinary powers were given to General Franklin Lucero, the commander of the army, and every effort seemed to be made to appease the military leadership. On the other hand, Perón also moved to try to get at least a truce with his civilian opponents. On July 10 he gave a speech in which he pledged to dismantle the repressive apparatus of the regime. He announced that the objectives of the 1943 Revolution had now been achieved, and that it was time for reconciliation. He also officially resigned as president of the Partido Peronista. On July 15 he reorganized the cabinet and dropped Minister of Interior Angel Borlenghi, who was feared and hated by opposition leaders.

For the first time in many years, Perón offered to let the

leaders of the major opposition parties have access to radio and television to present their points of view and to make suggestions as to what direction the country should take. As a result, Arturo Frondizi for the Radicals, and other speakers for the other parties, were able to address the nation. In addition, he made other overtures to the Opposition leaders.

However, after a few weeks, Perón appeared to have regained his confidence. As a result, on August 31 a gigantic meeting of his followers was organized in the Plaza de Mayo, and Perón addressed the crowd from the balcony of the Casa Rosada. This speech was a fighting one. He called upon his supporters to ferret out traitors and opponents of the regime and to deal with them summarily. There were some reports that he turned towards some of the military men who flanked him on the balcony as he said these words. This meeting seemed to indicate that Perón felt that he had regained full control of the situation and that he intended to make no further concessions to his opponents, either in the military or among the civilians. On September 3 a new and very repressive decree establishing once more a "state of siege" was issued.

The Final Coup

However, on September 16, 1955, the second—and this time successful—coup against the Perón regime began. This uprising did not start in Buenos Aires, but rather in the provinces. In the south, at Bahia Blanca and at other bases, the navy proclaimed itself in rebellion and seized control of nearby areas, while elements of the fleet steamed in the direction of the capital. In Córdoba, the cadets of the Air Force Academy, together with some army elements and armed civilians, and led by retired General Eduardo Lonardi, seized control of the city, and also proclaimed the overthrow of the regime. In the northeast, General Pedro Eugenio Aramburu, the only general on active service to join the revolt, immediately raised the army units in the province of Entre Rios against the Perón government. In one or two other provincial cities, rebel groups also took control. However, the central part of the country, and most particularly Buenos Aires and its environs, remained firmly in the hands of the Perón government. There was little or no move there on the part of the army garrisons to revolt, although some groups of armed civilians did prepare to go into action when the moment was propitious.

General Aramburu, in a conversation with me many years later, argued that what brought Perón down at that point was a failure of nerve, not a military defeat. He maintained that if Perón had sent his forces into action to suppress the revolt, he would have been victorious; only the outlying parts of the republic were in revolt, their resources were severely limited, and Perón, having the bulk of the army still loyal, could have put down this insurrection.

However, he did not do so. One explanation offered subsequently was that Perón surrendered power to save the city of Buenos Aires and other cities along the Rio de la Plata from bombardment by the navy. By the time he gave up, the heavy ships of the fleet were arranged along the Plata estuary and were threatening to bomb first the oil depots in the vicinity and later the city of Buenos Aires itself, if the president did not resign. This became the more or less official Peronista explanation for Perón's surrender. His own explanation to me was that he got out to avoid a civil war which would have undone all that he had accomplished.

After several days of apparent hesitation, Perón finally took refuge on a Paraguayan gunboat which happened to be in the Buenos Aires harbor. Shortly afterward, he was allowed to go off to Paraguay, to begin his eighteen years of exile and peregrination. Shortly thereafter, General Lonardi arrived in the capital to assume the presidency.

Summary

The overthrow of Perón was the culmination of a crisis that had been developing for several years. This crisis was rooted in the economy, in the reversal of the situation that had existed in the late 1940s and had resulted in lowering once again the workers' standard of living. It was contributed to by the intensification of the dictatorial aspects of the regime, as well as by its actions in apparently abandoning its nationalist banners and in picking a quarrel with the Catholic Church, the influence of which was much greater among his supporters than among his opponents. Finally, the crisis culminated in Perón's own loss of the will to fight, whether for reasons of cowardice, as argued by his enemies, or out of fear of the damage a civil conflict would impose upon the nation, as he and his supporters maintained.

SEVEN

The Years in the Wilderness

When he boarded the Paraguayan gunboat in the port of Buenos Aires, Juan Perón began a period of nearly eighteen years of exile. He wandered widely, but never abandoned the hope that he would return to Argentina and to power. Although he was apparently definitively defeated, the Argentine people continued throughout the period of his exile to be divided between those who were still his supporters and those who were his bitter opponents. Almost no one in the country was neutral with regard to Juan Perón.

From Buenos Aires, Perón first went to Paraguay. However, that country's president, General Alfredo Stroessner, whose accession to power the year before had been supported by Perón, did not want to imperil his relations with the new government of Argentina, so he soon saw to it that Perón abandoned his first place of refuge.

In the years that followed, Perón spent periods in Venezuela, Panama, Nicaragua, and the Dominican Republic before taking up permanent residence in Madrid, the capital of Franco's Spain. There he remained, with slight interruptions, until he returned to his native country in 1973.

Perón was in the Spanish capital for almost fifteen years. His opponents spread the story that he lived there in great luxury. However, this was more fiction than truth. I visited Perón in his Spanish home in 1960. He lived in an upper-middle-class housing development on the outskirts of Madrid, in a home which was quite comfortable but certainly not luxurious. He had several servants; his house was protected by guards, presumably armed, and inside the house, too, there were several men who appeared to be bodyguards.

Isabel Martinez, to whom Perón was not yet married, was very much in evidence and was clearly in charge of the household, although I was not introduced to her. She was giving orders to the servants about the plans for the day.

Although Perón did not live in any particular magnificence while in exile, he undoubtedly had at his disposal very considerable sums of money. Although the specific facts will probably never be known, Perón was widely reported to have gained access, after considerable difficulty, to bank accounts which Evita had left in Switzerland. He used his financial resources mainly to finance the political activities of his followers back in Argentina. He was certainly not the kind of person whose chief concern was with accumulating a fortune, although he was by no means immune to the delights of the flesh. His principal passion was for power rather than money. It was logical that he should use whatever funds were at his disposal primarily to try to regain the power he had lost.

"Volverá!"

Throughout the time of Perón's exile, he and his followers kept alive the idea that the ex-president would return to Argentina and to power. No matter how absurd this idea seemed at any particular moment, the Peronistas kept it alive. Sometimes this insistence even had comic overtones. In mid-1956, less than a year after Perón had been ousted, my wife and I were promenading in the Plaza de Mayo in front of the presidential palace. Suddenly, two pickup trucks sped around the streets surrounding the Plaza, and young men in the rear of the trucks threw thousands of copies of a throwaway to the crowd, then disappeared up the Diagonal Sur. Almost everyone rushed to pick these up, including my wife and I. The throwaways had at their top in large letters, "Volverá!" This idea that "he (she or it) will return" immediately caught one's attention, and the "he" was thought to be Perón. However, if one read on, one found that this was an advertisement for a furniture store, and that what would return was a bargain in the things the store had to sell! Most of the emphasis on "Volverá," however, was more serious than this. The rank and file Peronistas never gave up hope that their exiled leader would return to the country and that he would once again become president.

However, many political leaders, both supporters of Perón and his bitter opponents, were by no means sure either that Perón would come back or that he really wanted to do so. There were at least a fair number who felt that Perón had the best of both worlds—living in Madrid in comfortable circumstances but still maintaining the loyalty of a substantial part of the Argentine population—without running the risks that surely would be his if he were to return to Argentina.

Perón made one more or less serious effort to go back to his native country. In December 1964 he boarded a commercial airliner destined for Buenos Aires, but with intermediate stops in Brazil. When the plane arrived in Rio de Janeiro, Juan Perón was removed from it, held in custody for a few hours, and then was placed on a plane headed back to Madrid. There is, of course, an obvious question about how serious Perón was on this occasion about returning home. A well-publicized voyage on a commercial aircraft was hardly a method of return that had any high possibility of success. He certainly had resources at his disposal that would have made it possible for him to obtain an airplane for his own use to take him back to Argentina surreptitiously. One must conclude that this thwarted "return" was more a gesture designed to keep his followers convinced that he really did want to go back, than a serious effort to do so.

Varying Attitudes of Governments to Perón

During the eighteen years that Juan Perón remained in exile, most of the governments which were in power in Argentina dedicated a large part of their efforts to seeing to it that Perón would not in fact return to his native country, and certainly that he would not return to power. The military was, until the last years, completely dedicated to these ideas, and most of the non-Peronista civilian politicians were too.

Each successive regime adopted a somewhat different tactic to prevent the return of Perón. General Eduardo Lonardi, his immediate successor, adopted the slogan that "There Are Neither Victors Nor Vanquished," and his objective was to win Perón's followers away from him. He felt that if the corruption and tyranny of Perón could be made clear to those who had followed him, they would abandon his movement. The Lonardi government gave great publicity to the fortunes piled up by Perón and particularly by Evita. The regime suppressed the Peronista and Feminine Peronista parties, but allowed the CGT to continue under Peronista leadership. However, it required that there be elections in all unions within six months in the hope that, as a result of these elections, the labor movement would come to be controlled by anti-Peronistas and by younger Peronistas who had had no personal contact with, and had somewhat attenuated loyalty to, the exiled president. Deprived of the support of the labor movement, the Lonardi logic ran, Perón would have lost his political base in the country.

Lonardi's successor, General Pedro Eugenio Aramburu, took a quite different approach. Upon seizing power from General Lonardi, Aramburu was faced with a revolutionary general strike by the Peronista-controlled CGT—something that the same organization had not launched to keep Perón himself in power. As a result, Aramburu "intervened" virtually all of the country's labor organizations, including the CGT itself, placing military men in charge of the various unions. Although this might have been justified as a short-run measure, in view of the strike against the new regime, the Aramburu government continued this military intervention for two years or more.

Furthermore, President Aramburu's labor minister, Raúl Migone, had little knowledge of the realities of the Argentine labor movement, and as a result followed policies which tended to restore the faith of the rank and file workers in Perón, rather than alienating them from him. Migone sought the will-of-the-wisp of trying to "depoliticize" the labor movement, as a result of which he refused to work with any of those Socialist, syndicalist, and ex-Peronista labor leaders who might have been able to meet the Peronistas on their own grounds and defeat them. In addition, he staffed the Ministry of Labor with "bright young men" from the personnel departments of the country's largest industries. The net result of this was that the workers became convinced that they could get little or no help from the two organizations to which they had been able to turn during the Perón government. The unions were headed by military men, most of whom had little idea of what was needed to be a labor leader, while the Ministry of Labor was in the hands of the very people with whom the unionists had to deal across the table as representatives of their employers.

President Aramburu admitted to me in an interview many years later that because of the nature of his government's labor policies, he had done more to restore the workers' faith in Perón than Perón could ever have done himself. However, he added that he was a military man, that he had known nothing about labor problems, that he had had to depend on advice he received from his civilian friends, and that generally this advice had been wrong.

One other event of the Aramburu period alienated the workers from those who were opposed to Perón. This was the way in which the attempted military coup against the Aramburu government in June 1956 by elements loyal to the exiled president was handled. A handful of officers and enlisted men of the army, and some civilian supporters of Perón, were the participants in this effort. The uprising was suppressed with comparative ease, but the government then executed many of those who had participated in it. Those shot summarily, without virtually any kind of formal trial, included a general, Juan José Valle, other officers, some non-coms and some civilians. In all, over forty people were reported to have been executed.

The effect of this bloody aftermath of the Peronista revolt was very important in embittering the Peronistas. Figuratively, it drew a line of blood between the Peronistas and their opponents. It made it much more difficult for there to be any kind of reconciliation between those who were supporters of the exiled president and those who were his bitter opponents.

The Frondizi Government's Policy

The approach of President Arturo Frondizi, who took office as the result of elections in May 1958, was quite different from that of either Lonardi or Aramburu. When he took office, Frondizi was convinced that two major tasks faced his administration: to get the development of the Argentine economy going once again, and to bring about the reincorporation of the Peronistas into the regular political process. Basically, Frondizi's approach was to try to absorb the Peronistas into his own following, even being willing to merge his Intransigent Radical party into some new grouping which would include the great bulk of the Peronistas. Both his longer range economic policies and his political strategy were oriented towards this objective.

Frondizi's situation was rather unique. During the Peronista regime he had been the one important leader of the Opposition who had recognized that Perón had earned the support of the majority of the Argentine workers because he had done much on their behalf. He rejected the idea of opposing everything Perón did just because Perón did it, which was the attitude of virtually all of the other major anti-Perón leaders. Rather, he expressed general approval of the social and economic policies of the Perón government, although sometimes suggesting that they did not go far enough. He concentrated his attacks on the oppressive political aspects of the Perón regime.

Subsequent to Perón's fall, Frondizi also had a different attitude from that of the majority of the country's political leaders. Instead of lecturing the Peronista workers on how mistaken and misguided they had been to support Perón, he sought to establish as close relations as possible with the Peronistas. Lawyers of his Radical party faction became the primary attorneys for the large numbers of Peronistas— including virtually all who had served in the national or provincial legislatures—who were arrested and prosecuted during the Aramburu period. The Frondizistas raised money to aid the families of many of these people. Frondizi and his associates established contacts with the underground Peronista leadership. The result was that Frondizi had gained considerable sympathy among the Peronista masses. As we shall see later in this chapter, this was one of the major factors which convinced Perón to support Frondizi in the 1958 election campaign.

In terms of his long range economic policies Frondizi's program had several coincidences with that of Perón. He laid major stress on industrialization. He also accepted Perón's conviction that the government oil firm, YPF, could not by itself adequately develop the country's oil resources, and worked out a program to involve foreign oil firms in this sector, while avoiding the extremes of the kind of concession Perón signed with Standard Oil of California.

In the political field, Frondizi allowed the legal establishment of Peronista and "neo-Peronista" parties on a provincial level, although he did not legalize the Peronista party on a national basis. His hope, apparently, was that many rival Peronista factions would appear, under the circumstances in which, as a result of his own past performance and current policies, Frondizi was winning the support of the largest group of Peronistas. The first elections under these circumstances, held in 1961, seemed to indicate that Frondizi's policies were working. The Peronista parties did relatively badly, and his Intransigent Radical party made significant gains.

However, Frondizi became over-confident. As a result of the 1961 elections, he withdrew support from a bill pending before Congress to have congressional elections on the basis of proportional representation instead of the system in use since 1913, which provided that the party in any province that captured the most votes obtained two-thirds of the deputies, while the second most successful party gained the other one-third. Frondizi's error in judgment became clear in the March 1962 election. In that contest all seats in the Chamber of Deputies, as well as the governments of ten provinces, were at stake. This time the Peronista voters returned to their old habits and elected Peronista governors in six of the ten provinces—including the largest, Buenos Aires—and elected forty Peronistas to the Chamber of Deputies. Had proportional representation been in effect, the Peronista successes, at least in the Chamber, would have been significantly smaller.

This election provoked a crisis with the military, who were not willing to see Perón's followers regain control of key provinces and obtain the largest representation in the lower house of Congress. After some days, this crisis resulted in Frondizi's overthrow.

From Frondizi to Lanusse

Frondizi's downfall was followed by a year and a half of great instability. José María Guido, who had been president pro tem of the Senate, served as president of the Republic, and there was a struggle between factions of the military, which resulted at one point in a three-day civil war. Elections were finally held, from which the Peronistas' candidates were completely barred, and the victor was the nominee of the anti-Frondizi Peoples Radicals, Arturo Illia, who won with less than 30 percent of the total vote in a very split field of candidates.

Illia's policy towards the Peronistas was one of virtually doing nothing. Early in his administration the Peronista-controlled unions sought to launch what they called a "battle plan" in protest against the Illia government's economic policies. This consisted of a mounting wave of partial and general strikes, the obvious purpose of which was to force a showdown with the government that, hopefully, would provide the Peronistas with more martyrs and would perhaps convince the military to depose Illia. However, the president refused to react. He let the strikes occur, made no attempt to stop them, and finally in frustration the Peronistas called off their campaign.

However, Illia fell for the same reason Frondizi did. There were elections—again for ten provinces and all of the Chamber of Deputies—scheduled for March 1967. It was clear that if these elections were held with any semblance of honesty, the Peronistas would repeat their success of March 1962. This time, the military did not wait for the election to be held, they overthrew the president at the end of June 1966, thus obviating the need for holding the election.

The principal figure in the armed forces leadership, General Juan Carlos Ongania, succeeded Illia, and stayed in office for about four years, ruling by decree since he immediately dissolved Congress. He at first tried to appease the Peronista leaders, particularly the trade unionists, but in March 1967 had a major showdown with them, in the process of which he removed legal recognition from some of the most important unions and seized their property. He appeared for a while to have broken the back of the Peronista political and trade union apparatus. However, this appearance was deceptive. In mid-1969 there occurred the so-called *Cordobazo,* which we shall discuss more fully in the next chapter. This wave of strikes and riots marked the resurgence of trade union militancy, inaugurated a wave of left-wing terrorism, and sealed the doom of President Onganía.

About a year after the Cordobazo, Onganía was ousted, and in his place the generals placed the Argentine military attaché in Washington, Brigadier General Roberto Levingston. However, Levingston's hold on power was precarious, and in March 1971 the general who really controlled the military at that point, and who had chosen Levingston as president, General Alejandro Lanusse, deposed his nominee, and took over the presidency himself. With the inauguration of Lanusse there began the tortuous and complicated process of allowing the return of Perón, with which we shall deal in the following chapter.

Perón, the Puppeteer

Throughout all these years of coups, countercoups, and alternating policies on the part of successive governments, Perón continued to manipulate his followers from afar. He countered the policies of each regime in turn, contributing much to the failure of all of them. He succeeded in making Argentina virtually impossible to govern. In the following pages we shall sketch the nature of Perón's maneuvers.

Perón kept in constant touch with the political leaders of his movement and the trade union officials who represented the real core of the strength of Peronismo. He orchestrated and directed their maneuvers, he dictated their attitudes towards successive regimes, he played off one leader against another, one group of his followers against another, making sure that he kept the final control of the Peronista movement in his own hands. In the later years Madrid became a Mecca, towards which streamed not only innumerable Peronista leaders—to receive encouragement, instructions, praise and blame—but also many politicians who had never been Peronistas but who hoped somehow to develop a relationship with the exile which they could turn to their own advantage back home.

The first clear indication of the continuing hold which Perón had on a large segment of the Argentine people came in an election the Aramburu government called in 1957 for members of a convention to write a new constitution. At this time, from his exile Perón called upon his followers to cast blank ballots, not to support any of the many contending parties. The result was a triumph for Perón with 2,063,000 or 25 percent of the voters following his instructions.

The Constitutional Assembly proved to be abortive, making no substantial changes in the Constitution of 1853, which had been declared back in effect after the overthrow of Perón. The next step was to hold general elections in February 1958. This time, Perón was faced with a more difficult problem.

There were several presidential candidates, but only two of them stood a chance to win. These were the nominees of the two factions of the Radical party that many months earlier had split to form the Peoples Radicals, led by Ricardo Balbin, and the Intransigent Radicals, headed by Arturo Frondizi. Balbin and Frondizi were the respective candidates in the 1958 election.

Perón had two principal options at that time. He could either once again order his followers to abstain, or he could instruct them to vote for one of the candidates who was running. He did not have the choice of telling them to vote for a Peronista or near-Peronista candidate, because none of this description was allowed to run. In view of his success in getting his followers to cast blank ballots the year before, Perón may have been tempted to instruct them to do so again. However, several factors militated against this idea. One was that his followers were certainly becoming tired of having no influence at all on national politics. They wanted to make their weight felt in some way, and Perón was thus under considerable pressure to throw his and their weight in one direction or another. The second factor, as we have already noted, was that Frondizi had won considerable sympathy in the previous two years and more among the Peronistas. Furthermore, Frondizi was making an open bid for their support, promising substantial wage increases if he was elected, and promising to turn the unions, specifically the CGT, over to elected officers, which in effect by that time meant turning them over to the Peronistas.

Hence, Perón was under great pressure to back Frondizi. Also, secret contacts were made by Frondizi with Perón, soliciting his backing. The consequence was that only a few days before the election, Perón ordered his supporters to vote for Frondizi. This support was of great importance to Frondizi, not because it gave him the victory, which he probably would have had in any case, but because it made his margin of victory large enough so that those military men who were opposed to his taking office had little justification to offer for preventing his inauguration.

Perón's own explanation for why he backed Frondizi differed from that which I have offered here. In a conversation with me in 1960, he started off with the comment that "Balbin is an idiot," and went on to say that if Balbin had been elected he would not have stayed in office six months. He added that Frondizi would then have remained as a hope for the Argentine people. Frondizi, he said, was much more clever than Balbin, but he too would sooner or later be overthrown. At that point, Perón patted me strongly on the knee and asked the rhetorical question, "And then who will remain as the only hope of the Argentine people?"

These considerations may well have entered into Perón's calculations. However, he certainly also had to consider that his influence would suffer a severe blow if, without his endorsement, his followers had voted in large numbers for Arturo Frondizi.

In the election of 1963, won by Arturo Illia, the Peronistas were again not allowed to put up any candidate, and several who were successively endorsed by Perón were not allowed to run. At this time Perón and Frondizi formed an informal alliance, which in one way or another was to persist until Perón's death. Both ex-presidents called upon their supporters to cast blank ballots on this occasion, but the response was a disappointment for both Perón and Frondizi, since only about 18 percent in all did so.

It is not entirely clear to what degree Perón worked out all of the details of the strategy of the Peronista labor leaders—who controlled the CGT from about 1960 on—in their dealings with successive governments. However, the indications are that he was quite influential in this regard. He was constantly being visited by the more important labor leaders, and it was almost certainly he who worked out the general lines of strategy, although he may have had somewhat less to do with their tactical application.

Throughout all of these years, until the advent of Lanusse, Perón had to conduct his maneuvering without benefit of any direct contact with the military leadership that had the last word in the policies of all of the governments of the period. All of his supporters had been purged from the armed forces after his fall. Until the early 1970s the military leaders were virtually unanimous in their determination that Perón would never be allowed to come back to Argentina, let alone be allowed to return to power. Their only disagreements were concerning how these things were to be prevented. Throughout the period, the leaders were faced with the problem that any real return to political democracy, in which all elements would be allowed to participate freely, would almost certainly result in a victory of the Peronistas, in the face of the much-splintered opposition to the deposed president.

Although the trade unionists formed the core of Perón's support and much of Perón's contact with his supporters was through them, the Peronista movement was broader than just the labor movement. Virtually from the first months after Perón's overthrow there existed a clandestine General Command of Peronismo operating within the country. It included the trade unionists, but also contained other people who had no connection with the labor movement. At any given time, as well, there was someone who was the titular leader of this General Command as Perón's personal representative in Argentina. After the Aramburu period he was usually publicly identified. Presumably it was through this individual, whoever he might be at any given time, that Perón spoke most authoritatively to his supporters.

Divide and Rule

One of the most outstanding aspects of Perón's behavior during the years in the wilderness was his quite deliberate policy of preventing the rise within the Peronista movement inside Argentina of anyone who might possibly represent a rival for the overall leadership of the movement. Whenever someone gave indications of assuming such importance, he was cut down by Perón, symbolically, and perhaps in one case, physically. There were at least three cases such as this that occurred during the years that Perón was in Madrid. These were the destruction of the political positions of Raúl Matera, Augusto Vandor, and Jorge Paladino.

Raúl Matera was one of the first people to be publicly identified in the early 1960s as head of the Peronista General Command and Perón's personal representative in Argentina. He was a medical doctor who apparently had considerable talent as a political maneuverer and who succeeded in maintaining friendly relations not only with the other Peronistas but also with non-Peronista elements in the political picture who might be useful to the Peronista cause.

However, by 1963 Perón apparently had become worried about the potentialities of Dr. Matera. In the process of the maneuvers preceding the 1963 election, there was an attempt to have him be the candidate agreed upon by the Peronistas and various other groups that were working with them. Perhaps it was the willingness of other elements to support Matera that worried Perón, giving him the impression that Matera was developing a political strength of his own that might be dangerous to Perón sooner or later. In any case, it was suddenly announced that Matera was no longer head of the General Command, no longer Perón's personal representative, and no longer even a member of the Peronista movement. Little was heard of him politically for a long time thereafter. He returned to the Peronista ranks years later as a relatively secondary figure, and was minister of health in President Campora's cabinet in 1973.

The most serious case of this kind of treatment of his subordinates in the Peronista movement was that of Augusto Vandor. He had emerged in the 1960s as the leader of the *Unión Obrera Metalúrgica* (Metallurgical Workers' Union), perhaps the key to Peronista strength in the labor movement. But Vandor was the one labor leader who was also in a broader sense a political leader. He maintained reasonably friendly relations with non-Peronista union leaders. He had a very attractive personality, was very intelligent, had a broader political perspective than that of the trade union movement as such. There was even some discussion in the middle 1960s that, if conditions some day would permit it, Vandor was the one Peronista political leader who in his own right might be capable of becoming president of the Republic. Such rumors, of course, were sins enough in the eyes of Perón. However, he had to be cautious in dealing with Vandor, because of the strength of his union and his general position of leadership in the labor movement, which by no means depended only upon his having the blessing of Perón. So Perón bode his time.

Vandor had for some time been concerned with the state of the Peronista movement. He felt that for its longer-run prospects, there were great handicaps on the political side of Peronismo remaining underground and its public face being seen almost solely through the behavior of its trade union adherents. He felt that there was need for establishing an open, legal, Peronista party, whatever name it might take. He also felt that it should be the leaders of this party who should have the day-to-day charge of Peronista political activity inside the country, although Perón should continue, in consultation with the leaders in Argentina, to lay down general lines of strategy. Vandor approached Perón with this idea, and he assured me several months later that he had had Perón's acquiescence in the establishment of such an open party. Vandor therefore undertook the task, and it had its first test at the polls in provincial elections in the province of Mendoza early in 1966.

In the meanwhile, however, Perón changed his position. He made known to his supporters his opposition to what had come to be known among many as "Peronismo without Perón." A group of trade union leaders, headed by José Alonso, secretary general of the CGT, announced their opposition to the new legal party and organized a group to which they gave the name *"Peronistas a los Pies de Perón,"* "Peronistas at the Feet of Perón."

A short struggle ensued between the Vandoristas and Alonso and his group. Vandor's influence, however, surpassed that of Alonso within the ranks of the CGT, with the result that Alonso was forced out of his position at the head of the labor movement. Nevertheless, in spite of having won a victory in the labor movement, Vandor lost in the broader political arena. The crucial factor was the Mendoza elections where the followers of Alonso organized a list of candidates to run against those of Vandor. Perón sent his wife, Isabel Martínez, to the country to support the campaign of the Alonso ticket; the government, happy to encourage a split in the Peronista ranks, allowed the broadcast of a recorded message from Perón endorsing the anti-Vandor candidates. The consequence was that the Alonso-backed ticket received more votes in the Mendoza election than that organized by Vandor, although both were far behind the number of votes received by the victorious National Democratic party. This was a very severe setback for Vandor.

A few months later the issue became for the time being more or less irrelevant, when the military overthrew President Illia and all political parties were outlawed. What might have happened if Vandor had still been around at the time General Lanusse put an end to the military dictatorship after seizing power early in 1971 we shall never know. Vandor was murdered in his office in the Unión Obrera Metalúrgica in June 1969 by gunmen who were never caught or identified. There were those who felt that Perón himself may have had something to do with Vandor's murder.

The third case of Perón's eliminating a possible rival was

that of Jorge Paladino. He was head of the Peronista General Command and Perón's personal representative at the time that Lanusse seized power. He played a very important part in the early negotiations between President Lanusse and Perón (which we shall discuss in the next chapter). In the process of these negotiations, he received a significant amount of publicity, and gave considerable evidence of being a man of political sagacity and personal attractiveness. However, before the actual return of Perón, he had been removed from his position and had been expelled from the Peronista movement, for reasons which remain obscure.

The unwillingness of Perón to have around him or in his following people who had any independent power base, or who had prestige that went beyond whatever position Perón may have given him, was a fatal flaw in Perón's policy during his years in the wilderness. It meant that when he returned to power as an old and sick man he had no one within the ranks of his own movement who could truly be a collaborator and not just a puppet. It also meant that there were no figures who had any possibility of being his successor as head of the Peronista movement, who could give it the leadership and political direction that was so crucial once he had passed from the scene. By being so jealous of his position as the undisputed and unchallengable head of Peronismo, Juan Perón had destroyed the possibility of leaving behind a movement that could perpetuate in his name the things he had achieved and that could have assured him the positive position in history he undoubtedly thought that he deserved.

Summary

For almost eighteen years Juan Perón lived physically in exile and politically in the wilderness. During most of this time the military men and the civilians who ran the successive governments of the time had as their lodestar the vetoing of Perón's return to Argentina and to power.

Yet, through all of this period Perón kept his grip on the imagination and the loyalty of a large part of the working class, a fact that was due at least as much to the errors and shortsightedness of his opponents as to his own brilliance and ability, or even his own past record. From abroad he maneuvered among the various tendencies that were working to keep him away, ably manipulating the loyalty of his followers and the institutions that were controlled by them. The shadow of Perón thus lay over the country throughout the period. His followers never forgot him and his opponents could never be assured they would succeed in keeping him from returning.

Perón's ability in mobilizing his followers and maneuvering against the Opposition cannot be gainsaid. However, in historical perspective his behavior in this period may well appear self-defeating. His insistence on his personal return to power at all costs made any compromise between Peronistas and anti-Peronistas impossible. At the same time, his unwillingness to permit the formation of a Peronista political group with leaders of its own—although with continued loyalty to him—overshadowed his success in other directions. It is yet to be seen whether this fatal weakness has not left a vacuum and led to an end of Peronismo as a force in Argentine public life.

EIGHT

The Return to Power

In retrospect, it is clear that the chain of events which ultimately brought Juan Perón back to Argentina and then back to power, began in May and June 1969. The Cordobazo that took place then brought into the Argentine political picture a kind of civilian violence that had not existed before and began the process of convincing the military that it had failed in its most recent attempt to govern the nation, and that it would have to turn power over to an elected successor, even if he might be Juan Domingo Perón.

The Cordobazo and Its Aftermath

What the Argentines still call the Cordobazo was a widespread movement of protest against the economic and other policies of the military government of President General Juan Carlos Onganía. Although it was centered on Córdoba, it also took place in Rosario and several smaller cities.

The Cordobazo began as a series of student and workers' strikes. These had the support of most of the important unions in Córdoba as well as of the principal student organizations. They were also backed by the underground Peronista movement as well as by various radical groups that had some degree of influence in Córdoba organized labor, particularly the Trotskyites. Strikes became demonstrations that turned into full-scale riots. In fact, the movement in Córdoba, Rosario, and one or two other places took on the character of a full-fledged insurrection against the Onganía government. The army was called in to suppress the movement and it took several weeks for the military to completely put down the uprising.

Although the government was finally able to reestablish law and order, the long-run impact of the Cordobazo was very serious. As a direct result of it, one of the several Argentine Trotskyite groups, the *Partido Revolucionario de Trabajadores* (the Revolutionary Workers' party) decided shortly afterwards to launch a paramilitary organization, the *Ejército Revolucionario del Pueblo* (ERP—Revolutionary Army of the People), to carry on sustained armed conflict—that is, a terroristic or guerrilla campaign, depending on how one wishes to describe it. The idea of substituting terrorism for work in the unions and other mass organizations by no means had the unanimous support of the Partido Revolucionario de Trabajadores. The organization split, and the group opposed to guerrilla warfare ultimately joined with a left-wing faction of the Socialist party to form the *Partido Socialista de Trabajadores* (Socialist Workers' party). However, the terrorist faction of the group (the ERP) began a serious campaign against the government. It conducted a considerable number of operations during the next few years, which included the kidnapping of a number of important business executives and a large-scale raid on a naval air base. In the process of its operations the ERP acquired millions of dollars through bank robberies and the collection of ransom.

However, the ERP was by no means the only terrorist (or guerrilla) group that was established after the Cordobazo. Several others professing to be Peronista also began campaigns of kidnappings, murders, bank robberies, and other urban guerrilla activities. The most important of these was the so-called *Montoneros*, which by the time the Peronistas returned to power had absorbed most of the others.

The advent of the ERP, Montoneros, and other similar groups meant that a new element had appeared in Argentine politics. Hitherto, opposition to the status quo and the government in power had been confined to political agitation, strikes, and occasional demonstrations and riots. However, no civilian group had resorted to the deliberate and continued use of armed force.

Perón's attitude towards this new development was equivocal. He did not frankly endorse urban guerrilla activities and the deliberate, sustained use of violence, but he did not repudiate it either. He was particularly reticent about denying connection with those terrorists like the Montoneros who claimed to be his supporters. He sought to maintain their loyalty without alienating other elements that were opposed to terrorism.

However, after the Cordobazo it was clear that the nature of the struggle for power in Argentina had changed. The fact was that the terrorists, or guerrillas, became a permanent part of this struggle. Furthermore, they enjoyed wide sympathy among the general population. There were many people who were willing to give them refuge, or who were willing to help them in other ways in their struggle against the increasingly unpopular military regime.

The Expansion of Peronismo

The beginning of deliberate and sustained paramilitary activity against the government was not the only change in the Argentine political situation taking place under the Onganía government. Another highly significant factor was the growth of sympathy for Perón among groups which had traditionally been hostile towards him.

The bulk of Perón's backing since 1943 had come from the workers, particularly the organized workers. During Perón's long period in exile they had been the ones who had stuck with him through thick and thin. In contrast, during his first period in power, specifically from 1943 to 1945 and for many years thereafter, the middle class with the exception of some industrialists had been generally hostile to Perón. This was particularly the case with the university youth, who from 1943 to 1955 constituted the shock forces of the opposition to Perón and showed little sympathy for him after he fell. However, by the late 1960s this situation had begun to change dramatically. Perón began to rally strong support among the university students, and the *Juventud Peronista* (Peronista Youth), consisting largely of university and secondary school students, became a mass organization for the first time.

The change was rapid and dramatic. This was brought home to me in a conversation I had in 1972 with Rodolfo Puiggros, a Communist leader of the early 1940s who had subsequently led a minority of his party to support Perón and later still had become one of Perón's close advisers. (Throughout the ex-president's years in exile Puiggros had been well known as one of Perón's chief supporters among the intelligentsia.) In this conversation, Puiggros recounted to me the change he had encountered in the political atmosphere in the universities. He commented that whereas until shortly before our discussion he could not go near any of them for fear of being baited or even physically molested, he had suddenly begun to receive so many invitations to speak to groups of university students that he could not possibly accept them all. The students were anxious to hear about Perón, to know Puiggros' interpretation of what he stood for in Argentine national life, and to show their sympathy and support for the ex-president.

Like university youth throughout Latin America, the Argentine students had been fascinated by the Cuban Revolution, by Fidel Castro, and by Ernesto (Che) Guevara, who was a native of Argentina. However, at the same time they tended to be Argentine nationalists, and therefore not particularly prone to follow or be led by foreigners. Further-more, after the failure of Guevara's attempt to organize a rural guerrilla band in Bolivia—which resulted in his death—the Argentine students undoubtedly had grave doubts about the efficacy of his prescription for the rural guerrilla as the road to power, particularly in their own country. The students therefore tended to look for some other symbol and source of leadership for the struggle against the status quo, the bungling but all pervasive control of the military over political life, and the stagnation in the national economy. What was close at hand was Juan Perón and the movement loyal to him. So these students attached themselves to Peronismo, giving its doctrines their own particular twist and interpretation.

Perón welcomed these new recruits, despite the fact that they presented Perón with problems as well as with opportunities. His new young supporters had nothing but contempt for the well-entrenched trade union bureaucrats who represented the core of Perón's political support. Perón encouraged them to think that he shared their revolutionary ideas, but at the same time maintained his strong ties with the trade unionists, whose objectives were limited to the possible return of Perón to power and to themselves receiving a share in that power.

The Lanusse Government's Maneuvers

Although General Alejandro Lanusse gave as one of the reasons that he overthrew his predecessor the argument that President Levingston had sought to make overtures to Juan Perón, President Lanusse soon set about to do the same thing, much more openly and determinedly than had Levingston. General Lanusse's motives for this were undoubtedly mixed.

On the one hand, it is clear that he and those closest to him had come to the conclusion that in the light of the Cordobazo, the growing guerrilla movement, and the crisis in the nation's economy, it was high time for the military to turn over control of the government to elected civilians. Although he doubtlessly hoped that this would not be to Juan Perón or one of his followers, he became increasingly willing even to pay that price in order to get the military out of an increasingly impossible situation. It is also probably true that President Lanusse hoped that, in the process of the maneuvers leading to the return to constitutional government, he would emerge as the logical candidate for the presidency and would be elected. Like many others before him, he must certainly have dreamed of the possibility of striking some agreement with the exiled dictator that would bring Perón to throw his sizable following behind a friendly but non-Peronista candidate, in this case Lanusse himself. However, Lanusse was to be sadly outmaneuvered by the man in Madrid.

Soon after seizing power, Lanusse announced that he was going to prepare the way for elections and the installation of a new constitutional regime. He announced that the political parties, which had been outlawed by Onganía, would be allowed to reorganize, and that a new electoral law would be enacted. The Peronistas, of course, immediately raised the demand that they be allowed complete freedom to participate in these elections with whatever candidates they chose to run. They also demanded that the proscription of Juan Perón be lifted and that he be allowed to return to Argentina.

There then began a long series of maneuvers—the complete details of which probably only ex-President Lanusse is aware. Messengers went back and forth in a constant stream between Perón and Lanusse in the Casa Rosada. Perón's own followers made numerous pilgrimages to Madrid. Leaders of hitherto anti-Peronista parties did the same. The public process of preparing for the forthcoming elections took place against this semi-secret background of maneuver and negotiation. Little by little, Lanusse was forced to make concessions to Perón and his followers. The criminal charges which had been lodged against Perón right after his overthrow were withdrawn. His expulsion from the army was canceled. Lanusse announced that Perón was free to return to Argentina any time he wished to do so. The government disclosed where the body of Evita Perón had been buried—in a cemetery in Italy—and permission was given for it to be turned over to Perón and ultimately to be brought back to Argentina for burial there. The Peronista party was given legal recognition under the name *Partido Justicialista.*

As one of the final ploys in his maneuvering, President Lanusse had written into the new electoral law a provision that no one could be a candidate in the coming elections who was not a resident of Argentina by August 1, 1972. He thus hoped to force Perón to decide whether or not to come back and be a candidate, or perhaps to throw his support to Lanusse. Perón ignored this maneuver. He stayed in Madrid beyond the deadline, and thus ruled himself out, apparently, as a candidate. But he made a strong point of the fact that he was not thereby endorsing anyone else.

For his part, Perón carried out a maneuver a bit later, the exact purpose of which still remains somewhat obscure. He returned to Argentina in November 1972, three months too late to be a candidate, but nonetheless presenting Lanusse with a very ticklish problem. The government did nothing to prevent his return, and Perón spent about four weeks "holding court" in a well-guarded house in suburban Buenos Aires. Those four weeks were memorable and very important for the short renewal of his presidency that Perón was to enjoy a few months later. He was of course waited upon by his trade union and political followers of all kinds. However, he also received leaders of most of the hitherto anti-Peronista parties, most notably Ricardo Balbin, leader of the *Unión Cívica Radical del Pueblo* (Peoples Radical party), the most important non-Peronista party in Argentina at that time. He conferred with Balbin several times, and it would appear that a friendship was struck between the two men, who nonetheless remained political rivals.

It is not at all clear what Perón sought to achieve by this temporary return to Argentina. Perhaps he felt that by presenting President Lanusse with the fait accompli of his presence in the republic he could force him to revise the electoral law and allow Perón to be a candidate after all. Perhaps his main objective was to talk at length with non-Peronista political leaders and to convince them that if he returned to the presidency he would come back with a new spirit, a desire for national reconciliation. Whatever his purposes, Perón did not this time stay permanently in Argentina. He returned to Madrid, and soon after leaving Buenos Aires announced that the Partido Justicialista would have as its candidate in the coming election Hector Cámpora, one-time president of the Chamber of Deputies during the Perón administration of the 1940s and 1950s.

Cámpora was a most unexpected and even unlikely choice. At that time he was thought of an a nonentity, one who had never shown any real qualities of leadership and who had been a mere puppet of Perón during his service in Congress. In fact, the first reaction of many of Perón's trade union supporters was that they would have nothing to do with a Cámpora candidacy. It took several weeks to bring them around to a more or less whole-hearted endorsement of Perón's choice.

Meanwhile the election campaign went forward. A coalition was formed, the *Frente Justicialista de Liberación* (Frejuli—Justicialista Liberation Front), of which the Partido Justicialista was the core but which also included ex-President Arturo Frondizi's *Movimiento de Integración y Desarrollo* (MID—

Movement for Integration and Development) and splinters of the Conservative, Christian Democratic, and Socialist parties. Vicente Solano Lima, a dissident Conservative, was chosen as Cámpora's running mate. Frejuli backed Cámpora and Solano Lima for president and vice president, and had joint lists of candidates for the Senate, Chamber of Deputies, and provincial legislatures and governors.

There were eight other presidential candidates in addition to Cámpora. The most important of these was Ricardo Balbin of the Peoples Radical party, and the others included several brands of Trotskyites, a coalition of miscellaneous groups of which the Communist party was the most important, a candidate of the Democratic Socialist party, and several others. If President Lanusse had hoped that he would be a candidate to succeed himself, he was sorely disappointed. No party nominated him and his role was confined to seeing to it that the elections went off smoothly and fairly.

It was generally expected that Hector Cámpora would win the largest number of votes. However, the electoral law decreed by Lanusse provided that in order to win, a candidate would have to get at least 50 percent plus one vote, and that if this did not occur, there would be a run-off between the two candidates with the most votes. When the ballots were counted, Hector Cámpora had slightly more than 49 percent of the votes, but not the required half plus one. However, Ricardo Balbin, the runner-up with 21 percent, immediately announced that he conceded victory to Cámpora and that he would not take part in any runoff election. As a result, Cámpora was proclaimed president-elect. The Frejuli coalition also won a majority in the first Congress which Argentina had had since Onganía had seized power almost seven years before.

The Cámpora Presidency

Hector Cámpora was inaugurated as the country's second Peronista president on May 25, 1973. One of his first acts was to proclaim an amnesty for those who had been jailed for terrorist activities. He then set about rather energetically developing an economic and social program for the new government.

In a message to Congress shortly after taking office, Cámpora indicated a variety of measures that he would be sending for their consideration. To deal with the inflation problem, he proposed to reduce some prices, to freeze all the others, to permit a 25 percent general wage increase (that could not be passed on to the consumers), and then to freeze wages for two years. To get the economy moving he suggested an extensive public housing program, tax reform, reduction of interest rates, and development of a more efficient marketing system. He also promised legislation to regulate meat and grain exports, control foreign investment, nationalize bank deposits, and redistribute unused rural land. Before leaving office, Cámpora sent to Congress bills to nationalize bank deposits, to tax heavily unused land (both of which were passed during the interim regime after his resignation), and a measure defining the limits of foreign investment in the economy. Also. as an interim measure, Cámpora influenced the CGT and the CGE to agree to a Social Pact, freezing prices and wages for the time being.

Some new initiatives were taken in foreign policy under Cámpora. Diplomatic relations were restored with a number of Communist countries. A commercial agreement was signed with Cuba, under which the Argentine government agreed to finance some $200 million worth of Cuban purchases of Argentine products, principally manufactured goods, including automobiles and other vehicles over a period of several years.

Without doubt, however, the most spectacular event that occurred during Hector Cámpora's short presidency was Juan Perón's definitive return home. He arrived on June 20, 1973, and more than a million people went out to the environs of Eseiza Airport to receive him. However, the event was marked by a major tragedy, which bode ill for the future. Before Perón's plane had arrived at the airport, shooting broke out among the immense crowd that was waiting to receive him. The exact cause or sequence of the outburst of gunfire remains obscure, but what is certain is that various rival armed groups of Perón's supporters began shooting at one another. This caused a panic and in the mad rush many were trampled to death. At the same

time, infuriated members of the crowd lynched a number of
those who had done the shooting. The situation was so bad that
it was decided to have Perón land at a military airport in the
vicinity instead of at Eseiza. From there Perón was rushed into
Buenos Aires before the waiting crowd even knew that he had
arrived in the country. This tragedy put a pall on Perón's
return, which had been widely heralded as "The National
Reencounter."

With Perón's return to the country a situation developed that
was certainly embarrassing for President Cámpora. It was
summed up in one of the election slogans that had been widely
diffused during the campaign: "Cámpora President! Perón to
Power!" With Perón's return, there were in fact two presidents,
one in the presidential palace, another in Perón's apartment in
the outskirts of Buenos Aires. This situation did not last for
long. On July 13 Hector Cámpora and Vicente Solano Lima
resigned as president and vice president, respectively. This
move was obviously made to pave the way for the return of
Perón to the presidency.

The circumstances surrounding the resignation of Cámpora
and his vice president remain somewhat obscure. It is by no
means clear whether the original arrangement between Perón
and Cámpora had been that the latter would be a caretaker
president until the way for the return to the post by Perón could
be arranged, or whether Perón forced Cámpora out of the post
without there having been any such earlier agreement. In any
case, Cámpora's presidency lasted less than two months.
Chamber of Deputies President Raúl Lastiri took over as acting
president of the Republic.

With Cámpora's resignation, the country entered into
another presidential campaign. The list of candidates this time
was shorter, with a number of those who had run earlier in the
year endorsing the candidacy of Perón. Again, Ricardo Balbin
of the Peoples Radical party was the most important opponent
of the Peronista candidacy.

Perón was only presented with one significant problem
during the campaign. This was the decision concerning who
should be his running mate. His supporters were divided into
two broad camps, each of which in turn had its own sub-

factions. These two main groups were the traditional Peronista trade unionists and the groups that had adhered to his banner only since the late 1960s. Almost certainly, if he were to choose someone clearly associated with either of these two elements, it would arouse distrust and opposition from the other.

He was also faced with the fact that, as we have noted in the previous chapter, during his years in exile he had jealously prevented the rise of any figure who might possibly represent a challenge to his own authority within Peronismo. As a result, when he needed one in 1973, he had no person who was his indicated successor as head of the Peronista movement, who could as vice president be in a position to take over as president if he would not be able to serve out his full four-year term, as was certainly not unlikely (he must have known that the possibility was much greater than this).

It was against the background of these two factors that he had to make his choice of a vice presidential candidate. His first idea was to offer the nomination to Ricardo Balbin. However, the Peoples Radicals rejected the offer. So Perón selected his wife, Isabel Martínez de Perón. She had no close alignment with any faction within the Peronista movement and was only clearly associated with him. She had the added advantage for many of Perón's followers that she evoked the memory of an earlier Sra. de Perón, the "martyred" Evita.

The ticket of Perón and Perón won overwhelmingly. It received 62 percent of the vote, with Ricardo Balbin, the nearest opponent, getting 24.5 percent with the remainder of the vote being split among several minor candidates.

The Second Government of Juan Perón

It seemed almost as if the Juan Perón who returned to the presidency in October 1973 was a different man from the one who had abandoned it eighteen years earlier. Perón came back into office amidst a wave of national reconciliation and good feeling that was remarkable and would certainly have been thought of as inconceivable only a few years before. He had the enthusiastic support of a solid majority of the population. At the same time, the major elements of the Opposition were more

than willing to give Perón a second chance, and hoped
fervently that he would live out the four years of his new term of
office. Only a handful of his most obdurate opponents were
still completely unwilling to forget the past and continued in
their posture of unremitting opposition.

The only element of the Opposition to which Perón did not
especially make overtures was his opponents in the armed
forces. Both during the Cámpora and Juan Perón administrations, moves were made to cleanse the military of strong
opponents of Perón and to reinstate his ousted armed forces
supporters. A number of particularly hostile officers were
forced into retirement, while all of those officers who had been
ousted from the armed forces as Peronistas between 1955 and
1973 were restored to the service, with appropriate compensation. However, none of Perón's former enemies in the armed
forces were submitted to any treatment more severe than that of
having to end their military careers rather more rapidly than
they had planned.

Perón had great need for the support of his followers and the
tolerance of the Opposition, because his new administration
was faced with a large number of exceedingly difficult
economic and political problems. The Argentine economy had
been making little or no progress since the end of the Frondizi
administration, more than a decade before. The pent-up forces
of inflation were exceedingly great. Although the crops of
the year 1973 were good and their prices were acceptable,
the country still had substantial problems with its balance
of payments. In the political arena there was the la-
tent explosiveness within the Peronista ranks between his
traditional supporters and the Johnny-come-latelies of
Peronismo.

Perón sought to use the new era of good feeling to deal with
the country's most severe immediate economic problem, the
menace of inflation. The Cámpora administration's price
freeze on essential consumer goods and the CGT-CGE Social
Pact had worked reasonably well on a short-term basis, but
something more was needed to give the government a chance to
come to grips with the nation's intermediate and long-run
economic problems. However, Perón did not adopt a long-run

anti-inflationary program before he died, and by that time the Social Pact was beginning to wear thin. Unfortunately, Perón also gave relatively little attention during the few months of his second presidency to the other long-range problems of the national economy. No programs were presented to rehabilitate agriculture or to stimulate further industrialization. Little significant legislation went through Congress during this second presidency of Juan Perón.

One economic matter to which Perón did pay considerable attention was the effort to attract foreign investment, particularly from Europe. Before returning to Argentina he had conferred at length with a number of European (especially Italian) entrepreneurs, and he hoped to capitalize upon these contacts after he returned to the presidency. However, nothing concrete had resulted from the continuing negotiations before Perón's death.

Much of his time was taken up with political problems. Even before he was inaugurated, he was forced into a position of having to choose between his traditional labor supporters and those who had joined the ranks of his movement only in recent years. The problem had been present throughout the short Cámpora administration. Soon after Cámpora had taken office, the Juventud Peronista had presented Cámpora with a list of "demands" that it insisted he must carry out. This move irritated Perón, who summoned to Madrid the head of the Juventud Peronista, gave him a dressing down, and removed him from his position. At that point, the Juventud Peronista accepted Perón's rebuff with good grace. The removal of the head of the organization was followed by a large number of "self-criticism" sessions by local units, in which the young Peronistas admitted their "mistakes" and reaffirmed their loyalty to Perón.

The problem of the guerrilla or terrorist movement also had continued under Cámpora, and was one of the first things that Perón had to deal with upon taking office. With the election of Cámpora, those terrorist groups professing loyalty to Perón had announced that they were ending their guerrilla activities. However, after some internal discussion, the Trotskyite Ejército Revolucionario del Pueblo (ERP) announced that they were going to continue their activities. Nonetheless, their operations were considerably curtailed for several months. Since they no longer enjoyed any degree of public sympathy, and did not have the cooperation of the Montoneros and other Peronista groups, it was necessary extensively to reorganize the basis of their activities.

On September 25, two days before Perón's election, the terrorist issue was dramatized by the murder of José Rucci, Peronista head of the Confederación General del Trabajo. Although it was never determined exactly who had killed Rucci, Perón took this event as a direct challenge to him from those inside and outside his ranks who were trying to make it their revolution rather than his. As a result, even before taking office, he had acting president Raúl Lastiri outlaw the ERP, and Perón made a number of speeches roundly denouncing terrorist activities.

Subsequently, Perón moved strongly against leftist elements within the Justicialista ranks. The police raided the head-quarters of the Peronista Youth. Then, after first bringing pressure on various state governors to remove leftist elements from their administrations, he endorsed the ouster of the Leftist Peronista governor of Córdoba after that official had been removed by right-wing Peronistas and the police in March, 1974.

Perón's reaction in this situation was understandable. Faced with what he saw as the need to choose between those who had been loyal to him throughout his long period in exile and those who had joined his cause only recently, between those who had their own ideas about which way the new Perón administration should go—ideas that did not necessarily square with his— Perón quite comprehensibly decided in favor of his longtime supporters.

In spite of Perón's growing moves to curb the influence of the Peronista Left, it is significant that as long as he remained president, the Peronista Left did not break with him. Both the Montoneros and the Juventud Peronista continued to pledge their loyalty to Perón as long as he lived.

Perón's Death

Perón had come back to Argentina a very tired and sick man.

Even the official posters welcoming him back confirm this. Although showing his hair still black, they pictured the deep wrinkles in his face and his hardened, leathery, complexion. The smile they presented seemed forced and one might even think that it barely concealed pain.

In retrospect, it seems likely that Perón knew that he was a dying man when he took office in October 1973. Perhaps this knowledge was one factor in bringing about the conciliatory attitude that he adopted towards the non-Peronista part of the population just before and during his second period in office. He sought as a parting gesture to bring about a reconciliation in the body politic, to end once and for all the deep split among the people he had brought about almost a quarter of a century earlier. He wanted to leave to history the memory of a man who had forged national unity rather than one who had rent it asunder.

During the months of his second presidency there was a great deal of worry about his state of health. He was forced on various occasions to cancel appointments and to take to his bed for short periods of time. Rumors circulated constantly concerning the seriousness of his illness. The worries about Perón's health were probably as great or greater among the Opposition than among his own followers. Accepting as genuine his gestures of reconciliation and his promises to govern democratically, the Radicals in particular saw Perón as probably the only person with enough popular support to be able to lead the country through the terrible economic crisis that all admitted it was facing. They hoped (and prayed) that he would live long enough to overcome this crisis, thus laying the basis for establishing democratic constitutional government on a firm basis. They hoped that he could bring to an end at last the seemingly uninterruptible sequence of coups and counter-coups, a sequence that Perón had helped to start as a young army officer thirty-three years before, and for which he had borne so much responsibility, directly or indirectly after 1943.

Although it became widely accepted that he would probably not live out the full four years of his term of office, it nonetheless came as a real shock to the people of Argentina when, on July 1, 1974, it was announced that President Juan Domingo Perón had died. He was succeeded by his widow, Isabel Martínez de Perón.

NINE

Perón's Impact

Juan Domingo Perón unquestionably had great ambitions for his country and for the role that he and his country would play in the world. He wanted to diversify and modernize the Argentine economy, and he sought to right many of the nation's social wrongs. He aspired to make Argentina the leader of the countries of Latin America. He dreamed of carving out for himself an important role as the spokesman for a third force in world politics.

When he died, he had accomplished little of this. Although he had perhaps been the first Latin American since Simón Bolívar to draw world-wide attention and to make his name a household word, he left Argentina in the depths of an unequalled economic crisis, facing a political situation that threatened to deteriorate into civil war. In addition, by the time he died, Argentina was at the nadir of its influence in the hemisphere, had lost definitively the race for power and prestige with its traditional rival Brazil, had become the butt of jokes, and was the prime example of what other countries should *not* become.

Since Perón dominated the political life of his country between the coup of June 4, 1943, and his own death on July 1, 1973, he must to a large degree be held responsible for what happened to Argentina during these years. It is the purpose of this short final chapter to try to explore some of the ways in which he was responsible, and to try to reach a historical assessment of his influence on his country and the Western hemisphere.

Perón's Basic Economic and Social Objectives

We have argued throughout this book that on his way to power and in his exercise of it, Perón had a grasp of the economic and social necessities facing his country. He was correct in feeling that for Argentine economic development to continue, the nation had to follow a deliberate policy of going beyond being merely an exporting and importing nation, and had to launch a program of import substitution industrialization. He was right, too, in thinking that something had to be done about the country's social problems, and specifically about the conditions of life and labor of the Argentine working class.

To a considerable degree Perón succeeded in his objectives in these two fields. After his first period in office it was very difficult for anyone to argue any longer that Argentina was naturally destined to be only a grower of grains and a raiser of cattle and that any attempt to industrialize was "artificial." Nor was it possible any longer for the labor movement to be ignored or social legislation to be considered unimportant.

Perón's difficulties in the economic and social field were not in the basic policies which he launched; they were that he went too far in some of his economic policies. Although he made the labor movement a force in national life, he aligned it with a dictatorial regime and imbued its leadership with a tradition of opportunism and cynicism that still persists. There is little question, as well, about the fact that, in following the basically correct policy of transferring resources from agriculture and grazing to the industrial sector, Perón went too far. In spite of the industrialization program that he was pushing, Argentina continued to need the foreign exchange engendered by its rural exports. Yet Perón endangered the country's ability to obtain this, stimulating a retrogression in agriculture and grazing from which the country has still not recovered.

Furthermore, as we have noted earlier, Perón wasted a large part of the resources that were diverted from the rural sector. They were used for buying second-hand baubles for the military and for lining the pockets of favorites of the regime. The transfer of resources to bank accounts in Europe was on a sufficient scale to constitute a real impediment to Argentine economic development.

The result of the perversions of what was essentially a sound economic policy was that by the early 1950s Argentina was launched into an economic crisis that, with the exception of the four years of the Frondizi regime, has gotten steadily worse ever since. Foreign exchange shortages, uncontrollable inflation, stagnation of development, and the deterioration of the nation's social capital have been some of the contours of this crisis.

In the labor movement, too, a basically good policy was given a disastrous twist. By forcibly eliminating all leadership from the labor movement except that which was totally subservient to him, he and Evita developed a personal association of organized labor involving his political fortunes that in later years resulted in its suppression and persecution that was political rather than social. Also because of Perón's own lack of a clear political philosophy and his frequent substitution of maneuver for maneuver's sake in the place of principle, this too-close association of organized labor with Perón bred a kind of cynicism among the labor leaders that often degenerated into pure gangsterism.

Perón's Bid for International Leadership

In international affairs, Perón's grasp exceeded Argentina's reach. Argentina was a relatively narrow base upon which to depend for a bid for world or even Latin American leadership. Even this base shrank disastrously with the onset of the economic crisis in the early 1950s. In retrospect, it is clear that the kind of hemispheric and world leadership to which Perón was aspiring would not have been accessible to any Argentine president. Furthermore, Perón did not have available (had he wished to use it) the alternative possessed a few years later by Fidel Castro who, after vainly attempting to build an independent base of world and hemispheric power in the 1960s, settled in the 1970s for a certain degree of world prominence in the role of very junior partner and tool of the Soviet Union. There were several reasons, involving both the USSR and

Perón himself that made this alternative unavailable to him. On the one hand, during the time that Perón was in power, the Soviet Union was not yet ready to undertake the kind of economic, political, and diplomatic support for a country in the Western hemisphere which it later gave Castro's Cuba. Indeed, it is questionable whether, if Nikita Khrushchev had foreseen the cost of his involvement in the Cuban situation, he would even have been willing to undertake it in the early 1960s. But there was an additional reason why, even if the USSR leadership had been willing to make a large investment in some American country, that country would not have been Perón's Argentina. The Soviet leadership continued to remember Perón's sympathy for the Axis in World War II, and they continued to regard him as a Fascist, whom they could not support. Even the hysterical anti-Yankeeism of the earlier years of the Perón regime did not alter this judgment by the Soviet leaders.

The persistence of this attitude in Moscow was demonstrated in the behavior of the Argentine Communist party. At one point in 1952 when the principal figure of the party, Victorio Codovila, was in the Soviet Union for medical treatment and other matters, his temporary successor in the leadership of the party abandoned the strong opposition to Perón that had been the Communists' stance since 1943. He offered Perón "critical support." Thereupon Victorio Codovila hurried back from Moscow, reassumed his position at the head of the party, switched its policies back to hostility towards the regime, and disciplined his erring lieutenant.

The Question of Dictatorship

Certainly one of the basic elements during Perón's first period in power that historically served him most ill was his decision to govern as a dictator rather than as a democrat. If he had decided to govern democratically, he could probably have stayed in power (if not necessarily in office) as long or longer than he actually did. And he would not have dug the all but unbridgeable gulf in the Argentine body politic between Peronistas and anti-Peronistas which perturbed the nation's life for so long.

Perón's establishment of a dictatorial regime meant that one's attitude towards him and his government became the over-riding issue in determining where one stood in national politics. One's point of view on all other things was subordinated to this one consideration. Had Perón governed democratically, as it was quite within his power to do, political opinion could have divided on other issues: industrialization, economic nationalism, social reform. By no means were all of his opponents against his positions on these issues, but because of his dictatorship they could not join him in support of them. Not all of those enjoying the benefits of the dictatorship necessarily agreed with Perón's positions either, but the dictatorial nature of the regime gave them no option as to which camp they would have to be in.

The Years Out of Office

In the long years out of office, Perón went far towards destroying what he had been apparently trying to build during his first presidency. He did so in at least two ways: by making Argentina virtually impossible to govern, and by guarding with excessive zeal his position as the sole leader of Peronismo.

Throughout his almost eighteen years in exile, Perón insisted on only one thing: his own return to power. Over and over again, he mobilized his supporters against the regime in power, whatever it was. He converted the labor movement, which during most of this time was led by his followers, into an institution that was much more concerned with bringing back the ousted president than it was with improving the living and working conditions of its members. Until the penultimate moment, his insistence on his own return caused within the armed forces, which feared reprisals should he ever come back to power, an equally great insistence that he should never again be allowed to set foot in the national territory. He kept in existence the yawning gulf in public opinion between his supporters and his opponents. He made any kind of compromise that might have reintegrated his followers into national political life impossible. He thus assured the continuance of the unending series of coups and countercoups that marked the period from 1955 to 1971.

With the one end in view of returning to power, Perón was willing to accept support from wherever he could get it during those years. Regardless of what they were doing to the fabric of Argentine society, he refused to criticize any group that was undermining the regime that kept him out of power. Thus in the years after 1969 he led the guerrillas, both those operating in his name and those who were not, to feel that they had his blessing, a policy that was to rebound against him once he did in fact come back to the presidency.

Together with this absolute refusal to compromise on the issue of his return to power was Perón's truly disastrous policy of preventing the emergence of any independently based political leadership in the ranks of Peronismo. He would support only those who were unconditionally at his orders. He defeated the one serious attempt made by Augusto Vandor to establish a legal political party that, although loyal to Perón and willing to follow his direction on broad policy, would run its own affairs without day-to-day consultation with him. He destroyed politically all of those like Matera, Vandor, and Paladino, who acquired a certain degree of status in their own right, and he perhaps had Vandor physically disposed of. Of all of Perón's errors, perhaps this was the most serious one. It prevented the rise of a younger leadership in the Peronista movement, a leadership which might have assumed a major role even during his lifetime. This would have assured the continuation of Peronismo and of the policies he and Peronismo represented after he had passed from the scene.

The result was, of course, that when he needed such leaders to bolster his regime once he returned to the presidency, he did not have them. He had to rely on his wife, Isabel Martinez de Perón, a very weak reed indeed. She was a woman completely without political talent, a person who was hopelessly out of her depth when great responsibility was forced upon her, a figurehead manipulated by unscrupulous men who were little more than gangsters. But in Perón's eyes, she had one prime virtue: she was completely subordinate to him.

The Last Hurrah

When Perón finally did return to the presidency of Argentina, it was too late. He did not have a long enough time to live to be able to solidify the era of good feeling he obviously wanted to establish, to end once and for all the polarization between Perón/anti-Perón forces. He was already very sick; he survived less than nine months after reassuming the presidency.

Furthermore, Perón does not seem to have returned to power with any clear view of what was necessary to reestablish the health of the economy and thereby to provide a solid base for the regime. Although he had told me many years before that he knew that Argentina had easily exploitable national wealth, in 1973 to 1974 he showed no signs of understanding that what the country needed at that point was to facilitate the exploitation of that wealth by rapid rehabilitation of agriculture and grazing. With two or three years to increase agricultural output and to replenish the cattle herds, Argentina would have been able to beat the foreign exchange problem, to deal with its inflation, and to have a basis upon which to get the economic development of the country going again. Instead, Perón came back into power with the apparent intention of repeating once again many of the economic programs of his earlier period under conditions in which they were no longer really relevant.

Had Perón come back to power in good health, he probably would have had the reserves of popular support and good will sufficient to lead the Argentines through the two or three years of relative austerity that would have been needed to make it possible to carry out the program Argentina required. But he neither lived long enough for this nor had any clear idea of what kind of a program was needed, even if his health *had* been such as to get him over the years necessary to rehabilitate the economy.

The Things for Which Perón Was Not Responsible

There were, of course, a number of elements in the Argentine situation for which Perón was not chiefly responsible. For one thing, he did not start the succession of coups and counter-coups of post-1930 Argentina, although he did little to end the sequence and did much to perpetuate it during and after his first presidency. He was not responsible for the labor and other policies of the Aramburu administration which widened even further the Perón/anti-Perón chasm in public opinion.

Juan Perón was also not responsible on the international scene for the rise in power of Brazil, which tipped the balance of power and prestige in South America so markedly against Argentina. The rapid and nearly continuous industrialization and general diversification of the Brazilian economy, the push of that country into its interior, and a relative degree of political stability were the principal factors accounting for the expansion of the economic, political, and diplomatic strength of Argentina's northern neighbor. However, even here Perón, through the contribution that he made to bringing about the general stagnation of the Argentine economy, by making it virtually impossible after 1955 for any government to last long enough to develop an economic policy, helped to make the gap between Brazil and Argentina even greater than it would otherwise naturally have been.

Perón's Legacy

On balance, then, Juan Domingo Perón was unable to achieve the position in history to which he aspired. Instead of a country with a prosperous and expanding economy, he left one in the grip of an unprecedented economic crisis. Instead of a strong and stable government, he passed on a weak one. wracked by violence, and virtually without leadership. Rather than a people full of confidence in themselves and in their future, Perón left one torn by self-doubt, pessimism, and frustration. Instead of a nation of great prestige, with a voice listened to with respect in world councils, Perón's legacy was a country with less influence than it had at any time before in the twentieth century.

Juan Perón's failure was due in part to his lack of any clear political philosophy, which led him to substitute tactical maneuver for strategic objectives, and in a considerable degree was due to certain traits in his character. Over the course of his career, Perón's admittedly great talents as a politician were more often than not directed towards destruction rather than towards construction. His cynicism in manipulting people was in the long run self-defeating. The authoritarian tendency in his character that found expression in his activities as a politician, both when in and out of office, served to polarize the Argentine population for a whole generation. It prevented Perón from leaving the legacy of great achievement and a solid and well-led political movement that could carry this achievement on into the future. As a result, Juan Domingo Perón appears historically as more a tragic figure than a great one.

Argentine Presidents: 1916–1977

This table lists the Argentine presidents in the sixty-one years from 1916 to 1977. The period each of them served, how they took office, and how they left office is indicated.

President	Dates of Incumbency	How Assumed Office	How Left Office
Hipolito Irigoyen	1916–1922	Election	Election
Marcelo T. de Alvear	1922–1928	Election	Election
Hipolito Irigoyen	1928–1930	Election	Coup d'etat
General José F. Uriburu	1930–1932	Coup d'etat	Fraudulent Election
General Agustin P. Justo	1932–1938	Fraudulent Election	Fraudulent Election
Roberto Ortiz	1938–1942	Fraudulent Election	Death
Ramon S. Castillo	1942–1943	Succeeded as Vice President	Coup d'etat
General Arturo Rawson	June 1943 (2 days)	Coup d'etat	Pressure of Fellow Officers
General Pedro Ramirez	June 1943– February 1944	Pressure of Fellow Officers	Pressure of Fellow Officers
General Edelmiro Farrell	February 1944– June 1946	Pressure of Fellow Officers	Election
General Juan Perón	June 1946– September 1955	Election	Coup d'etat
General Eduardo Lonardi	September– November 1955	Coup d'etat	Coup d'etat
General Pedro Aramburu	November 1955– May 1958	Coup d'etat	Election
Arturo Frondizi	May 1958– March 1962	Election	Coup d'etat
José Guido	March 1962– October 1963	Coup d'etat	Election
Arturo Illia	October 1963– June 1966	Election	Coup d'etat
General Juan C. Ongania	June 1966– June 1970	Coup d'etat	Coup d'etat
General Roberto Levingston	June 1970– March 1971	Coup d'etat	Coup d'etat
General Alejandro Lanusse	March 1971– May 1973	Coup d'etat	Election
Hector Campora	May–July 1973	Election	Resignation
Raul Lastiri (acting president)	July–October 1973	Constitutional Succession	Election
General Juan Perón	October 1973– July 1974	Election	Death
Isabel Martinez de Perón	July 1974– March 1976	Succeeded as Vice President	Coup d'etat
General Jorge Videla	March 1976	Coup d'etat	

Interview with Juan Perón

Below are my notes written immediately after I had talked with Juan Perón in Madrid on September 1, 1960. The interview took place in the living room of Perón's house in the suburbs of the Spanish capital quite early in the morning, just after Perón had completed having breakfast.

As an interview subject, Perón was a disappointment to me. On several occasions when he was still president, I had sought to talk with him in the Casa Rosada, and when I had told anti-Perón friends about my efforts to get an interview, they had given me a warning. They said that Perón was an exceedingly convincing man in personal conversation, and that if I were not careful he would prove to me that black was white and vice versa. I found this not to be the case when I finally did get to talk with him.

My disappointment in this interview arises from the fact that Perón lied to me on a number of points. Since I had the opportunity to talk with him on the basis of the fact that I had written a book about him, I presumed that he would realize that I knew a fair amount about him and his career. It also seemed logical that, given these circumstances, he would not say things to me that I would surely know not to be true.

Nonetheless, this interview is of interest. It presents the picture which Perón wanted a foreign writer to have of him and of what he had done. It is thus of some significance in trying to assess Perón's career.

The notes follow.

*   *   *

The best people who worked with him in the Argentine labor movement were ex-anarchists who had come after the Spanish Civil War, like Santín. They were idealists. He likes to work with idealists better than other types, but in politics one must work with all kinds. With idealists one can do things for the good of the country. With others, they are interested only in things which are good for their own interests.

He had long been interested in social problems. His father had always instilled in him the need to emulate great men. In the army he had seen many young men of twenty years of age coming in as draftees who had no decent clothes, were barefoot. He saw the army reject many who were undernourished. He talked at length with many of these young draftees, who had not yet learned to lie, and who told him the truth about the backgrounds from which they came. Also in army service, he travelled widely throughout the country, and saw the miserable conditions of life and work which existed in many areas.

He was lucky to have been sent on a study mission to Europe between 1938 and 1940. He saw the great social movements that were in progress there in Italy, France, and Germany at that time. He did not get to Russia.

Out of all of these elements he developed his own social philosophy. He felt that humanity tended to be torn by two extremes: liberal democracy of the nineteenth century, and popular democracy that will be the hallmark of the twenty-first century. This is the century of great social transformations, the twentieth. He saw the need for developing an intermediary philosophy between liberal democracy and popular democracy. That is what Justicialismo is.

The Revolution of 1943 was caused mainly by the colonels. It was made because of the prospect of the election of Patrón Costas as president. The reaction in the army was against his extreme conservatism, not against his pro-British attitudes. He had an estancia in Salta where he had his own police, his own money, a veritable state within a state. The prospect of his coming to power was terrible. However, the 1943 Revolution was not a social revolution in the beginning.

Rawson became president by a fluke. The colonels forced

him to resign by threatening to chuck him out of the window of the Casa Rosada if he did not do so. Rawson was able to proclaim himself president because of the hesitancy of Ramirez. General Ramirez was no good—a slow-witted, unintelligent character who drank entirely too much.

Perón was vice president and minister of war. But he quit these two posts to head the Department of Labor, which he intended to transform into a Ministry of Labor. He did so, with the establishment of the *Secretaría del Trabajo*. In that post, he talked incessantly with union leaders and with the masses. The union leaders were in the majority Communist at that time. In one year Perón gave three thousand talks and speeches, with small groups or with large ones. He convinced the workers that he was on their side. Finally, when other officers realized the support that he had from the workers, they threw him out and jailed him on Martín Garcia. It was then that there occurred the general uprising of his followers. His wife played an important part in this uprising. Cipriano Reyes was just one of many trade unionists who participated in it. The result was that Perón was brought back from prison.

He fulfilled his promises to the workers; this is why five years after his ouster he is more in command of Argentina than President Frondizi and all of the generals are. He gave ten years of social justice, of peace and stability. The workers remember this very well.

His economic policies while president were very successful. When he was overthrown, the Banco Central had $700 million in foreign currency and $850 million in gold. He paid off all foreign debts, had a modest internal debt of 8 billion pesos. The budget was 18 billion pesos and was balanced. Agricultural production had increased under him from 6 million tons of wheat to 10 million. Argentina was a power in the world. It had one of the world's most solid currencies; the black market price of the dollar was 27 pesos.

The successor governments have dissipated all of this. All the reserves of foreign exchange and gold are gone. They were spent on buying airplane carriers, and he is sure that much was robbed. The foreign debt is now $2.5 billion, the budget is over 100 billion pesos and half of it is not covered by income. Wheat production is down to 5 million tons, of which Argentina consumes 3.5 million. The rest it cannot sell since the United States is giving wheat away. The peso has been up as high as 107 to the dollar.

But all of this can be restored quickly. Argentina is basically very rich. The government can restore the situation by consolidating the foreign debt on a long-term basis, can establish the price controls and exchange controls that he had in effect. There was no inflation during his period because prices were controlled by the government.

The situation in Argentina now is heading for chaos. If it does not come to that by itself, the Peronistas will cause chaos. It is heading towards civil war. Only the Peronistas are capable of managing chaos, as they showed after October 17, 1945.

The Communists are growing rapidly now. They had 130,000 votes before his regime. In the last election under him, they got only 30,000. Now they have half a million votes, in a few years they will have a million, then two million. Only he can stop the Communists; he is the only deterrent. Now he can stop the Communists in all of Latin America, but he does not know if he will be able to do so in six months' time. He did not suppress the Communist party. He does not believe that the way to fight the Communists is by suppressing them. Puiggros was never one of his advisers. He is a Trotskyite. Castro is symptomatic of what is going on in Latin America today. Perón has no alliance with Castro. They are moving in parallel lines at the moment. But he is too old a politician to fall into the trap of having an alliance with Castro.

He backed Frondizi for a very simple reason. If he had not backed Frondizi, Balbin would have won. Balbin is an idiot. That would have meant a return to office of the old conservative elements, while Frondizi would have remained as a hope for the country. He knew that Frondizi would be a failure, and would not carry out the program on which he was elected. So now who is the only hope for Argentina?

Frondizi is a scoundrel, a bandit. He has not the dignity required of a president of Argentina. He will do anything to remain in power, but he will not remain in power in spite of this for very much longer. Frondizi is very wrong if he thinks that some improvement in the economic situation will destroy the strength of the Peronistas.

It is not true that after World War II Argentina had vast foreign exchange reserves she was free to use. She had $3 billion in the United States, but for three years it was frozen, the U.S. authorities arguing that due to the changeover from war to peace industries, the United States could not provide the things Argentina needed. When it was possible to supply them, prices had risen in the United States so that Argentina was robbed of $2 billion of the $3 billion reserves that she had. As for the situation with regard to sterling balances, the British declared the inconvertibility of the pound, so that the Argentines could not use their dollars to buy in Britain or their pounds to buy elsewhere. Argentine credits in Britain were frozen, just as her dollar reserves were. So Perón scoured the world to buy war surplus. On one day, for example, Perón purchased 60,000 trucks. He bought much industrial machinery second hand. Much of it was old, but it improved the economy of Argentina. The purchase of the railroads was good business. It did not cost one centavo of Argentine reserves. They were bought with the equivalent of one year's supply of wheat to Britain.

Under Perón trade was conducted on the basis of bilateral barter. This has been abolished by the present government, with the result that Argentina now has a sizable trade deficit, which did not exist during the Perón regime.

The economic difficulties of Argentina since 1955 are due to the fact that under Perón there existed a perfectly working economic machine. Successor governments have taken this machine apart piece by piece, and now the economy is not functioning well as a result.

All revolutions that are real revolutions are a phenomenon of more than one generation. From 1900 to 1917 in Russia there was a period of propagation of the revolution; the period of Stalinism was the consolidation of the revolution; the period of Khrushchev is the period of institutionalization of the revolution. Perón represents the period of propagation of the Argentine revolution. It is still going on and will go on for a long time to come.

He has studied well the Italian fascist experience. He saw the weaknesses of its so-called corporate state. The corporations come from the Middle Ages, when social and economic functions joined with political ones. The French Revolution of 1789 separated these functions, giving social and economic functions to *sindicatos*, and political ones to parties. Mussolini tried to associate these functions, setting up sindicatos that had economic and social functions but he was never willing or able to give them political functions. The party, which was in essence the militia, would not permit the transfer of political functions to the sindicatos.

Perón was not going to repeat the failures of Italian Fascism. So he allowed the parties to function normally. In fact, what he wanted was two great parties, such as exist in the United States or Britain, one the Peronista Party on the left, with its big rival on the right. It is not true that he forbade coalitions of parties. The opposition parties did not coalesce in the 1951 election because they did not want to do so.

He built up the various confederations as centers of economic and social power. The CGT was for the workers, the CGE for all economic forces, the CGP for professional people, the CGU for students. In the new provinces the constitutions provided for equal representation of these groups with geographically elected members of the legislatures. Perhaps this would have come to the national government too, but he would not have imposed it, it would have come naturally if it had come.

He has never had anything against the United States. It was the United States that attacked him, as they attacked Franco. Perón opposed the attacks on Franco, which were wrong and unjust. The United States developed an economic blockade of Argentina under Truman. When Eisenhower came in, he changed this policy; he sent Milton down, who was a very reasonable fellow. So when the United States stopped being hostile towards Argentina, he stopped being hostile to the United States. He never had done anything concrete against the United States. For instance, he paid for IT&T's business in Argentina with cash. Many new investors came to Argentina from the United States during his regime, such as Squibbs and others.

He never got any loans from the United States. The

Eximbank (the U.S. Export-Import bank) loaned to private businessmen in 1951. The loan for the steel plant had not been concluded when he fell. The steel plant was built by German interests, who gave better terms than the Westinghouse Co., which wanted to do the job and whose representatives in Argentina were good friends of his. Perón said that he would cut off his arm rather than incur a new foreign debt for Argentina, and he lived up to this.

It is true that the Argentine army had great sympathy for the Germans in World War II. The Argentine army had been trained by the Germans since 1910. Faupel had been in Argentina before the war. Perón was very well treated by the German army when he was in Germany in 1938. But the Argentine army did not do anything to help the Germans in the war. It is not true that there were submarine bases there or that Faupel came there during the war. He came afterwards and died there.

The role of Evita was mainly in the social welfare field. Although Perón created a social security system covering illness and old age, there were always a number of people who were not covered, such as bums and orphans, etc. So Eva Perón created the Social Welfare Foundation. It had old folks' homes, orphans' homes, and schools with 60,000 children. It had a home for the families of the unemployed. It had a number of medical centers. The Foundation was financed exclusively by popular contributions, receiving no money from the government. Evita also was often approached by the unions for help in their welfare projects, but she played no other role with regard to the labor movement. Basically, Eva Perón died of overwork. He went to work at 6 a.m., at the time when she usually returned from work. She was a very good organizer and orator. She got leukemia, which is cancer of the blood.

It is not true that he suppressed the freedom of the press. *La Vanguardia* was published regularly through his regime, as was the Communists' daily paper. There were 600 Opposition periodicals during his regime. What he and his friends did do was to buy up a number of papers, which is certainly quite legitimate. Now, in contrast, there really is suppression of freedom of the press. All of his chain of papers were confiscated, and the Peronistas can not publish a paper there now, as the government will not allow it.

There has been a world-wide conspiracy of silence about the tyranny of the Frondizi regime. It maintains a concentration camp in the southern part of the country. The provisional government killed 2,000 people in the June 9, 1956, revolt. There are many political prisoners. The net effect of all of this is to strengthen the Communist party.

He personally had no trouble with the Church. But the Church clashed with the CGT because it wanted to establish a Catholic labor movement. The Church also clashed with the Peronista party because it wanted to establish a Christian Democratic party, thus putting the Church into politics. Perón was never excommunicated. This is a fable circulated around the world by the United Press, but it is untrue. An act of excommunication against the president of a republic must name him by name, but there is no such decree of the Vatican in existence. The two priests who figured in this, Tato and his friend, were not expelled from Argentina as they alleged. They were implicated in a revolutionary attempt that failed, and fled the country of their own free will. When they got to the Vatican, they said that they had been expelled and without investigating, the Vatican excommunicated "all those concerned with the expulsion" of the two. Now the Vatican, which is "infallible," cannot say that it made a mistake, so everyone there now denies any knowledge of whether or not Perón was excommunicated. He never expelled those two priests; in order to do so he would have had to sign a decree, and there is no such decree in existence.

He believes in God, and that God is superior to all human beings. But this does not apply to the Church or to its priests, who are fallible human beings like everyone else. Religion and the Church are not the same thing.

Relations with the army were always good. In 1951 a handful of officers, bought by the British who resented the loss of business resulting from Perón's industrialization program, revolted. But they were only a handful.

Relations with the navy were not so good. It was always opposed to the army. The same situation exists in the United

States. In 1955 he had deprived the fleet of all ammunition, but the British supplied it with munitions in the Islas Malvinas, and it was these they used in their revolt.

The tales of corruption in the Perón regime are all fables. Miranda had a fortune of 300 million pesos when he entered the government, and he owned thirty factories. When he left the government he had only one-tenth of this, because he had not been able to attend to his business. Jorge Antonio gained a fortune legitimately, being Mercedes-Benz representative and having other business. If he and others got contracts from the government because they were friends of Perón, this is natural, since he cannot be asked to give contracts to his enemies instead of his friends. When Edward Kaiser came to Argentina in 1953, he told Perón that he was in difficulty in the United States because of the change in administration, which had brought the General Motors Co. into a preferred position. Charges that Perón himself got rich are absurd. If he did, where is all his wealth?

He can legitimately attack military men in politics, because from the moment he became a politician, he ceased being a military man. He has no further interest in being a general.

He quit in 1955 because if he had not done so there would have been a civil war, that would have undone all that he had accomplished. He was not governing for Perón, but for the nation. If he had been governing for Perón, perhaps he would have stayed on and shot all the rebel generals. He felt that if he were right, he would come back, and if he were not right, he had no right to power anyway.

Bibliographical Note

The purpose of this bibliographical note is twofold. On the one hand, I wish to give an indication of the specific sources that I have used for this book. On the other, I want to suggest to those readers who wish to investigate more extensively the Perón phenomenon some other possible sources of information.

Much of the data and most of the judgments in this volume come from my own observations gathered in thirteen trips to Argentina over a period of thirty-one years, during the administrations of Juan Perón, Pedro Eugenio Aramburu, Arturo Frondizi, Arturo Illia, Juan Carlos Ongania, Alejandro Lanusse, Hector Campora, Isabel Perón and Jorge Videla. In these trips I had a chance to observe a great variety of different events. I have interviewed perhaps a thousand different people, many of them on frequent occasions. They include politicians of almost every variety, trade unionists, business men, military officers, priests, students, and foreign observers from several nations.

Four interviews have been referred to directly in this volume. These were with Juan Perón, which I had in Madrid on September 1, 1960 (my notes of which constitute Appendix B of this book); with Pedro Eugenio Aramburu, in Buenos Aires on June 7, 1968; with Rodolfo Puiggros, in Buenos Aires on June 10, 1972; and with the Chilean political leader, Eduardo Alessandri, in Santiago on June 21, 1972.

In the chapter on Evita I have quoted from two textbooks of the Perón period. One, for first graders, is entitled *Cajita de*

Música (Buenos Aires: Angel Estrada Editores, n.d.), and the other, a second grade reader, is *Bichitos de Luz* (Buenos Aires: Editorial Kapelasz, 1954).

Most of the books that have been written about Perón have dealt with his rise to power and his first period in the presidency. These include my own volume, *The Perón Era* (New York: Columbia University Press, 1951), which was perhaps the first overall study of the rise of Perón to appear in English; and George Blanksten's *Perón's Argentina* (Chicago: University of Chicago Press, 1953), which is particularly useful for trying to understand the concepts of Perón's supposed political philosophy, "Justicialismo." In the early 1950s, also, there appeared at least two studies of Evita. One was the very good book by María Flores (Mary Main), *The Woman With the Whip* (New York: Doubleday & Co., 1952). The other was the less useful volume of Fleur Cowles, *The Bloody Precedent* (New York: Random House, 1952).

Other volumes of interest were published in this early period when Perón was still in power. These included James Bruce's *Those Perplexing Argentines* (New York: Longmans, Green & Co., 1953), written by one of those who served as U.S. Ambassador accredited to President Perón, and *Nuestros Vecinos Justicialistas*, by the Chilean Christian Democrat Alejandro Magnet (Santiago: Editorial Pacífico, 1955), one of the best studies to appear in Spanish. The book edited by Joseph R. Barager, *Why Perón Came to Power—The Background to Peronism* (New York: Alfred A. Knopf, 1968), although being published much later, also deals with this early period in Perón's political career.

Several volumes have dealt with Perón's impact on the Argentine labor movement. My own book *Labor Relations in Argentina, Brazil and Chile* (New York: McGraw-Hill, 1962) sketches the labor relations system established under Perón; it also deals with the way in which the first post-Perón governments modified it. Sam Baily's book *Labor, Nationalism and Politics in Argentina* (New Brunswick, N.J.: Rutgers University Press, 1967) studies how and why the previously "internationalist" Argentine labor movement became "nationalist" under Perón. The unpublished Ph.D. dissertation by

John Deiner, *ATLAS: A Labor Instrument of Argentine Expansion Under Perón* (New Brunswick, N.J.: Rutgers University, 1969), is a very good study of Perón's use of the Argentine labor movement in his foreign policy.

There is one invaluable study of the role of the Argentine military, both before and during the early part of the Perón period. This is Robert Potash's *The Army and Politics in Argentina* (Palo Alto: Stanford University Press, 1969). It provides essential information on the origins of the 1943 coup d'etat and the years just after that, and I have drawn substantially on it in discussing Perón's rise to power.

There are also several studies of the relationship between the Perón regime and the Catholic Church. One which was published in Spanish soon after the fall of Perón was Ludovico Garcia de Loydi's book *La Iglesia Frente el Peronismo* (Buenos Aires: CIC, 1956). A more recent work is the unpublished Ph.D. dissertation of Noreen Stack, entitled "Avoiding the Greater Evil: The Response of the Argentine Catholic Church to Juan Perón" (New Brunswick, N.J.: Rutgers University, 1976). She argues that the Church was principally concerned with its own internal problems of adjustment to modern Argentine society during the Perón period and did not see itself as being committed either to the support of the Perón regime or to opposition to it.

There have been several attempts before Perón's return to power, and from several different points of view, to present an overall assessment of Perón's importance in Argentine history. One of these was Alberto Ciria's book *Perón y el Justicialismo* (Mexico City: Siglo Veintiuno, 1971), was sympathetic to Perón but was not an apology for him. Another was *El Peronismo* (Buenos Aires: J. Alvarez, 1969) by Rodolfo Puiggros, a Marxist-Leninist supporter of Perón. There are also Jorge Abelardo Ramos' *Perón: Historia de su Triunfo y su Derrota*, written by a one-time Trotskyite, sympathetic to Perón. Alberto Belloni's *Peronismo y Socialismo Nacional* (Buenos Aires: Editorial Coyoacan, 1962) is written from what is perhaps a more orthodox Trotskyite point of view.

There are relatively few studies of what has happened in and to Argentina since Perón's first presidency. One of these is

Arthur Whitaker's book *Argentine Upheaval—Perón's Fall and the New Regime* (New York: Praeger, 1956). Another is Roberto Cori's *Sindicatos y Poder en Argentina* (Buenos Aires: Editorial Sudestada, 1967), which is a study of the trade union movement during the Perón regime and the first decade or more after it was overthrown. My own book, *An Introduction to Argentina* (New York: Praeger, 1969) deals extensively with the governments after the Perón regime, particularly that of Arturo Frondizi.

So far as I know, the present volume is the only book written after Juan Domingo Perón's death that tries to assess his career, in perspective. Therefore, I have nothing further in this field to recommend.

Finally, note should be taken of the many publications of Juan Perón himself. During his first period in power many of his speeches were distributed in various languages as pamphlets. Subsequent to his overthrow, he wrote several books, defending what he had done and attacking his successors. After Peronismo was again allowed to come out into the open in the early 1970s, a flood of books by Perón appeared in Argentina. Most of these were collections of speeches, although some were more coherent volumes.

Index

control of Peronista parties, 59-60

"cult of personality," 59

destruction of the independence of the labor movement, 57, 79-82

died of cancer, July 26, 1952, 87

dissolved Sociedad de Beneficiencia, 82

established Eva Perón Welfare Foundation, 82

events of October, 1945, 45-46

eyes and ears of Perón, 79, 85-86, 105

forced newspaper owners to sell out, 55

gave away property of others, 83-84

La Razon de Mi Vida, 79

marriage to Perón, 78

myth of her "martyrdom," 88, 91-93

organized and ran spoils system, 79, 82-83

opposition of the military leaders, 77-79, 88

Perón's mistress, 77

received Latin American labor leaders, 72

relations with men, 77

reinforced Perón's popularity, 79, 86

rejected nomination as vice-presidential candidate, 88

request that she be declared a saint, 90-91

showing off her possessions, 84-85

Swiss bank accounts, 67, 98, 112

trip to Europe, 70

Perón, Mario (Juan Perón's father), 18

Perón, Mario (Juan Perón's brother), 18

Peronista parties (after Perón's overthrow), 117-120

Peronista party. *See* Partido Peronista

"Peronistas a los Pies de Perón," 125

"Peronistas at the Feet of Perón." *See* "Peronistas a los Pies de Perón"

Peronista Youth. *See* Juventud Peronista

Postal Savings Bank, 81

Potash, Robert, 24-25

Progressive Democratic party, 48

Puiggros, Rodolfo, 42, 132

Quijano, Hortensio, 42

Radical party. *See* Unión Cívica Radical

Ramirez, Pedro, 24-25, 29-35, 41

Rawson, Arturo, 31-32

Renovated Radical party. *See* Unión Cívica Radical Renovada

Revolutionary Army of the People. *See* Ejercito Revolucionario del Pueblo

Revolutionary Workers' party. *See* Partido Revolucionario de Trabajadores

Revolution of June 4, 1943, 1, 9, 11, 14, 17, 21, 24-26, 29-32, 36, 80

Revolution of 1930, 20-21, 25

Reyes, Cipriano, 38, 46, 48, 56, 60

Rio Treaty. *See* Inter-American Defense Treaty

Rivas, Nellie, 96

Roman Catholic Church
hierarchy supports Perón's candidacy in 1946, 49
open warfare between church and state, 103-105

Romualdi, Serafino, 101

Roosevelt, Eleanor, 86

Rosas, Juan Manuel de, 2-3, 53

Rucci, José, 142

Rural Society. *See* Sociedad Rural